HOW TO TRAVEL TO OTHER DIMENSIONS

An Eleven Lesson Course

On What You Will Find There!

DragonStar

and
S. Panhadasi

Inner Light Publications
New Brunswick, NJ 08903

HOW TO TRAVEL TO
OTHER DIMENSIONS

by Dragonstar and S. Panchadasi

Cover Art by Tim Swartz
Editorial consultant, Carol Ann Rodriguez

Timothy Green Beckley, Publisher

Request a free catalog from Inner Light Publications
Box 753, New Brunswick, NJ 08903
A free subscription to the Conspiracy Journal is available on the net at
www.conspiracyjournal.com
Credit card orders at 732 602-3407

How To Travel To Other Dimensions

DRAGONSTAR

INNER LIGHT PUBLICATIONS

CONTENTS

1

CONTENTS

Other Possibilities, Other Realities

IT wasn't that long ago that the suggestion that there were other dimensions, other parallel worlds besides our own, would have been met with derisive laughter and comments of "reading too much science fiction." However, here in the 21st century the "many worlds" interpretation of quantum mechanics is now widely accepted by scientists who are no longer afraid to openly discuss the amazing possibilities that this concept presents to us.

The origin of the "many worlds" conjecture is connected with quantum mechanics, a branch of physics that studies the infinitesimal world and predicts the behavior of nanoscopic objects. Physicists had difficulties fitting a mathematical model to the behavior of quantum matter because some matter exhibited signs of both particle-like and wave-like movements. For example, the photon, a tiny bundle of light, can travel vertically up and down while moving horizontally forward or backward.

Such behavior starkly contrasts with that of objects visible to the naked eye; everything we see moves like either a wave or a particle. This theory of matter duality has been called the Heisenberg Uncertainty Principle (HUP), which states that the act of observation disturbs quantities like momentum and position.

In relation to quantum mechanics, this observer effect can impact the form – particle or wave – of quantum objects during measurements. Future quantum theories, like Niels Bohr's Copenhagen interpretation, use HUP to state that an observed object does not retain its dual nature and can only behave in one state.

How To Travel To Other Dimensions

In 1954, a young student at Princeton University named Hugh Everett proposed a radical supposition that differed from the popular models of quantum mechanics. Everett did not believe that observation causes quantum matter to stop behaving in multiple forms.

Instead, he argued that observation of quantum matter creates a split in the universe. In other words, the universe makes copies of itself to account for all the possibilities and these duplicates will proceed independently. Each of these universes offers a unique and independent reality that coexists with other parallel universes.

If Everett's Many-Worlds Theory (MWT) is true, it holds many ramifications that completely transform our perceptions on life. Any action that has more than one possible result produces a split in the universe. Thus, there are an infinite number of parallel universes and infinite copies of each person.

If this is true, then is it possible to travel to one of these other dimensions, either with our minds, or even physically? Well, that's what this book is all about, as this idea is nothing new. Many great minds over the centuries have realized that our world is not alone, that there are many, many other worlds that can be accessed under the right conditions.

The first step in this amazing journey is to accept the reality of different dimensions. The multiverse is an infinite honeycomb of possible universes. You may be aware of only one universe right now, but there are other alternate dimensions...you just aren't aware of them yet.

Now is the time to cast aside your old ways of thinking and join the thousands of others who have learned to control their path through the mulitverse. Don't be afraid, the many worlds of reality beckon and with the right frame of mind they will soon be yours.

CHAPTER I.

THE SEVEN PLANES.

EVERY student of occultism, from the humblest beginner to the most advanced pupil, has a full realization of the wonders of that strange plane of being known as The Astral World. The beginner, of course, has not the privilege of actually viewing life on this plane, except, perhaps, in exceptional cases, or under extraordinary circumstances. But even he finds constant reference to the subject in the treatise his studies, and soon discovers that that particular plane is the scene and field of some very strange phenomena.

As he advances, and learns more of the occult laws and principles, he develops still greater interest in the subject. And, when he reaches the stage in which he is able to actually sense (by astral vision) on this plane, he finds that a new world of experience has opened out before him.

The oldest occult teachings, as well as the latest, inform the student that there are Seven Planes of Being. The lowest of these planes is that which is known as the Material Plane.

Second in order is that which is known as the Plane of Forces. The third is that which is known as the Astral Plane. The fourth is that which is known as the Mental Plane.

Above these four planes are three higher planes, known to occultists, but which have no names that can be understood by those dwelling only on the lower planes, and which are incapable of explanation to those on the lower planes. I shall refer to some of these higher planes, in this little book, as we proceed, but shall make no attempt to describe them for the reasons just given. Our subject for the present consideration is merely the Astral Plane, and we shall find sufficient interesting facts in considering the phenomena of that plane without attempting to penetrate the veils of those still higher.

It should be mentioned at this point, that each of the Seven Planes has seven sub-planes; and that each of these sub-planes has its own seven subdivisions; and so on to the seventh degree of subdivision. So, you see, there is a most minute classification in the occult teachings.

The student of occultism, at the beginning, usually experiences difficulty in forming a clear conception of the meaning of the word "plane" as used in the occult teachings. Consulting the dictionary, he is apt to get the idea of a plane as one of a series of straight layers— one part of a great strata—above and below which are other layers or strata. It usually is quite difficult for the occult teacher to eradicate this erroneous idea from the mind of his pupils, and to substitute the correct concept.

This error arises from thinking of these planes of being as composed of matter, or material substance, which, of course, is incorrect. When it is remembered that even the densest form of matter itself is composed of vibrations of energy (as recognized by modern science), and that the Forces of Nature are but manifestations of vibrations of energy, one begins to find the key. Instead of the planes rising one above the other in the scale of the fineness of matter, they are graded according to their respective degrees of vibration of energy. In short, they are planes of vibrations of energy, and not planes of matter at all. Matter is simply the lowest degree of vibrations of energy, that is all.

The second common source of error, on the part of the beginner in occultism, is that of picturing the planes as lying one above the other in space. This conception, of course, naturally follows upon the error of thinking of the planes as a series of layers or strata of fine matter; but it also often persists even after the student has grasped the idea that the planes are grades of vibration, rather than of matter. But, finally, the student is impressed with the idea that the planes are not "layers" or "strata" at all. The planes do not lie one above the other, in space. They have not spatial distinction or degree. They interpenetrate each other in the same point of space. A single point of space may have its manifestations of each and all of the seven planes of being.

Some of the old occultists sought to explain this condition of things to their students in the words of a very celebrated ancient teacher, who originated the aphorism: "A plane of being is not a place, but a state of being." No words can give a better explanation of, or aid, to, the correct mental conception of the idea of a "plane" in the occult sense of the term.

To those students who may find it difficult to form the idea of a number of manifestations, each having its own rate of vibration, occupying the same point of space at the same time, I would say that a little consideration of the phenomena of the physical world will perhaps serve as an aid in the matter. For instance, every student of physics knows that a single point of space may contain vibrations of heat, light of many shades, magnetism, electricity, X rays, etc., etc., each manifesting its own rate of vibration, and yet not interfering with the others.

Every beam of sunlight contains many different colors, each with its own rate of vibration, and yet none crowding out the others. By the proper laboratory apparatus each kind of light may be separated from the others, and the ray thus split up. The difference in the colors arise simply from the different rate of etheric vibrations.

Again it is possible to send many telegrams along the same wire, at the same time, by using senders and receivers of different vibratory "keynotes." The same thing has its corresponding analogy in the case of wireless telegraphy. So, you see, even on the physical planes we find many forms of vibratory manifestation occupying the same point of space at the same time.

The Material Plane, with which we are all familiar, has, of course, its seven sub-planes, and likewise its seven-times-seven series of subdivisions, as have all the seven planes. At first we are apt to think that we are perfectly familiar with every form of matter, but this is far from being the case, for we are familiar with only a few forms. The occult teachings show us that on certain of the fixed stars, and some of the planets of our own chain, there are forms and kinds of matter as much lower in vibration than the densest form of matter known to us, as these dense forms are lower than the highest ultra-gaseous forms of matter recognized by us. And, on the other hand, the same teachings inform us that there are in existence, in other worlds, and even (to an extent) in our own, forms and kinds of matter as much higher than these highest forms of ultra-gaseous matter known to us, as the said known forms are higher than the densest form of matter now known to us. This is a startling statement, but every advanced occultist knows it to be true.

Physical science formerly classified matter as follows: (1) solids; (2) liquids; (3) gaseous. But modern science has found many forms of matter far more tenuous and rarer than even the finest gas. It now calls this fourth class "ultra-gaseous matter." But occultists know that beyond this fourth sub-plane of matter which science is just now discovering, there lie three other, and still finer, sub-planes, of which science at present has no conception.

Next higher in the scale of manifested being, we find what is known as the Plane of Forces, of which very little is known outside of occult science, although, of later years, physical science has been breaking into this field. In the next twenty years physical science will proceed further in this direction. The research into radio-activity is leading toward further knowledge regarding this plane of manifestation.

On the Plane of Forces, we find the seven sub-planes, and likewise the seven-times-seven subdivision. There are forces far below the scale of the ordinary forces of Nature known to man. And, likewise, there are great series of Nature's Finer Forces at the other end of the scale, of which the ordinary man—even the scientist—knows nothing. It is these finer forces which account for many of the wonders of occult science. In particular, the fine force called "prana" or "vital force," plays an important part in all occult phenomena.

Next above the scale of the Plane of Forces, we find the great Astral Plane, the consideration of which is the purpose of this little book.

CHAPTER II.

ASTRAL REGIONS.

IN the occult teachings we find frequent references to what are called "the astral regions," and the inhabitants and phenomena of said regions. Like the term "plane," this term "region" has caused much misunderstanding. The old occultists used it in a loose sense, knowing that their pupils clearly understood the real significance. They did not care whether or not other persons understood. But the modern investigator, without the benefit of a teacher, often finds himself confused by this mention of "regions" of the Astral Plane, and frequently finds himself thinking of them in the sense of the "heavens and hells" of the old theology—as definite places in space. But these astral regions are nothing more than vibrational manifestations on the Astral Plane, which have no special reference to any set-aside portion of space, and which manifestations may, and do, occur at almost any point of space. The astral regions occupy the same space as the material regions, neither interfering with the other.

The term "astral" is derived from the Greek

word meaning "related to a star," and was originally used in describing the heavens of the Greeks—the abodes of their gods. From this sense and usage the term widened in application, until it was employed to indicate what might be called the "ghostland" of the ancient people. This ghostland was believed to be inhabited by beings of an etheral nature, not only disembodied spirits, but also angelic beings of a higher order.

The ancient occultists of Greece, and other Western lands, thus naturally fell into the custom of using the familiar term to indicate that which we know as the Astral Plane in modern occultism. Of course, the Oriental occultists had their own terms for this plane of manifestation, which terms were derived from old Sanscrit roots, and which were much older than the Greek terms. But, as the use of Sanscrit terms has a tendency to confuse Western students, the best Oriental teachers, today, in teaching Western students, almost always use the old Greek occult terms.

At this point, I must answer. a question which usually presents itself to the mind of the intelligent student at about this particular stage of the teaching. It is probably in the mind of the student who is reading these words, at this particular moment. The question may be stated as follows: "How is it possible for anyone to speak intelligently of the phenomena of the Astral Plane, if that plane is on a higher vibratory scale than the physical senses. How can one visit, and perceive things on, the Astral Plane, without his body being dematerialized?"

This question is a natural and perfectly fair one, and evidences the inquiring mind which the true occultist always possesses. And no true occult teacher will hesitate for a moment in frankly answering it. For, remember this always, my students, the occult teaching is not based merely on the principles laid down as "gospel" by the old occultists. Respect, yes! great respect is paid to these old teachings, of course, but every advanced occultist knows that he must actually experience the manifestation of occult phenomena before he can positively pronounce the same to be an occult truth. Such experience comes to every advanced occultist, when he reaches the necessary stage of development· which alone renders such experience safe for him. Like the scientist, the true occultist learns by his own experience, built upon the recorded previous experience of others. To the advanced occultist the phenomena of the Astral Plane is just as real—just as readily sensed—as is the phenomena of the material plane to those functioning upon it.

But, to answer the question: One does not have to disintegrate or dematerialize his physical body in order to visit or sense the Astral Plane and its phenomena. There are two avenues of approach to the Astral Plane, as follows: (1) by the employment of the astral senses; and (2) by visiting in the so-called "astral body." Let us consider each of these avenues in turn.

By the term "the astral senses," occultists indicate that wonderful secondary set of senses, corresponding in office to the five physical senses, by means of which man is able to receive impressions on the Astral Plane.

Each of the physical senses of man has its astral counterpart, which functions on the astral plane just as the physical senses do upon the material plane. Thus every man has, in latency, the power of seeing, hearing, feeling, smelling, and tasting, on the astral plane, by means of these five astral senses. Nay more, as all advanced occultists know, man really has seven physical senses instead of five, though these additional two senses are not sufficiently developed for use in the average person (though the occultist of fair attainment generally unfolds them into use). And even these two extra physical senses also have their astral counterparts.

In the cases of persons who, accidentally or through careful training, have developed the power of astral vision—perception through astral sight—the scenes of the Astral Plane are perceived just as clearly as are those of the material plane perceived by the physical sense of sight. The ordinary clairvoyant has flashes of this astral vision, as a rule, and is not able to sense astrally by an act of will. The trained occultist, on the other hand, is able to shift from one set of senses to another, by an act of will, whenever he wishes to do so. In fact, such occultists may function on both planes at the same time, in this way, if they so desire.

In cases of clairvoyance, or astral visioning, the occultist remains in his physical body, and senses the phenomena of the Astral Plane quite naturally or easily. It is not necessary for him even to enter into a trance condition, or any abnormal mental state or condition. And still less is it necessary for him to leave his physical body in such cases. In the instance of the higher form of clairvoyance, he may even sense events both on the physical plane, as well as the astral planes, at a distance—though, strictly speaking, this belongs to a somewhat different order of occult phenomena. To vision astrally, the occultist has merely to shift his sensory mechanism, just as the operator on the typewriter shifts from the small letter type to the capitals by a shiftkey. This, then, is the simplest and most common way of occult sensing on the Astral Plane. It is possible to many to whom the second method is impossible.

The second avenue of approach to the Astral Plane is that in which the individual leaves his physical body, and actually travels on the Astral Plane in his astral body. The astral body is composed of an etheral substance of a very high degree of vibration. It is not mere matter, and yet is not mere force—it is composed of astral substance which resembles very fine matter, but which is far more tenuous than anything that is known as matter. Ordinarily the astral body can be sensed only by means of the astral vision, but under certain other conditions it takes on the semblance of a vapory form of matter, and is perceptible to the ordinary physical senses as a "ghost" or "apparition," even when the person is in physical life.

The astral body is an exact counterpart of the physical body, but survives the latter by a number of years. It is not immortal, however, and finally disintegrates and is resolved into its original elements just as is the physical body.

The advanced occultist, in his astral body, is able to leave his physical body (which remains in a state of sleep or trance) and to visit at will on the Astral Plane, even at points in space far removed from his physical body.

He, however, is always connected with the physical body by a thin, cobweb-like, filament of ethereal substance, which extends or contracts as he travels away from, or toward, the sleeping physical body. If this filament is broken by an accident on the Astral Plane, his physical body "dies" and he is never able to return to it. Such accidents are rare, but occult history has records showing their occasional occurrence.

Many persons are able to travel in the astral body, during ordinary sleep, but usually have no recollection of the same upon reawakening. The occultist, on the other hand, travels consciously, and with a purpose, and always is wide-awake on such journeys. He is as much at home on the Astral Plane as on the physical one.

And so, student, you see how the occult teaching regarding the Astral Plane has been obtained; and how such teaching has as firm a basis in actual experience as have those based upon physical observation, experiment, and experience. Moreover, every occultist may verify the teaching for himself—in fact actually does so.

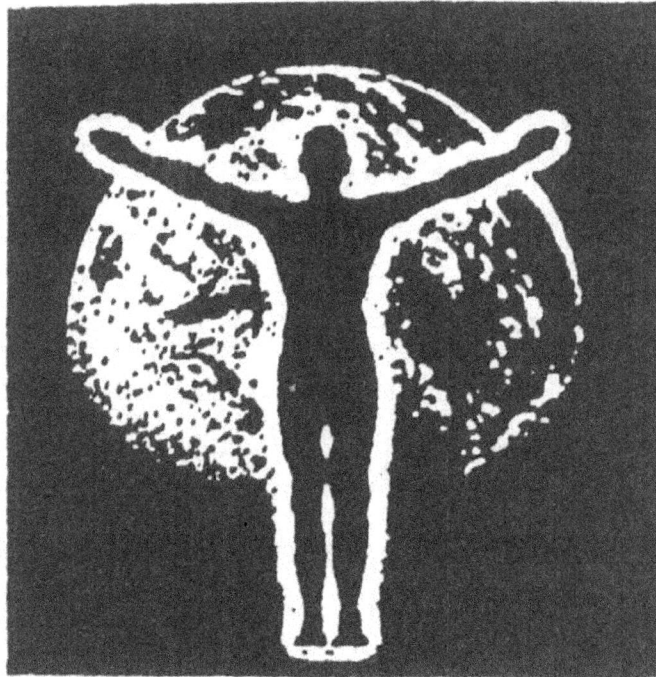

CHAPTER III.

REALITY OF THE ASTRAL.

IT is customary among occultists to speak of the Astral Plane, simply as "the Astral," as for instance "out in the Astral;" "visiting the Astral;" "phenomena of the Astral;" "inhabitants of the Astral," etc., etc. The student may as well familiarize himself with this use of the term "the Astral," in order to understand, and be understood by, others interested in occult study. Accordingly, I shall from now on use this term, "the Astral," as indicating the Astral Regions—the Astral Plane—without further explanation.

One of the hardest things for the elementary student to realize is that the Astral is just as real, abiding, and fixed as is the material world. Just as steam is actually as real as water, or even as ice, so is the Astral just as real as the world of the physical senses. For that matter, if we could see our world of matter placed under a sufficiently strong magnifying glass, we should perceive it not as a great body of solid fixed matter, but rather as an aggregation of an infinite number of the tiniest particles themselves built into atoms; these built into molecules; and these built into solid masses.

The space between the ions of the material atom is as comparatively great as the space between the planets of our solar system. And every ion, atom and molecule is in constant and intense motion. Under a glass of sufficient power, there would seem to be nothing solid in the material world. If the magnifying glass were to be raised to an infinite power, even the ions would melt into seething nothingness, and there would be nothing left but the ether which has no weight and which is imperceptible to the senses even when aided by the strongest instruments of the laboratory. So you see, the solidity of things is merely relative and comparative. The vibration of substance on the Astral is higher than those of the material plane; but even the Astral vibrations are far slower than those of the next higher plane, and so on.

To the traveller on the Astral the scenery, and everything connected therewith, seems as solid as the most solid material does to the physical eye. It really is just as solid as is the astral body in which you visit it, for that matter. As for reality, the Astral is just as real as is the material, in every respect.

The Forces of Nature are not perceptible to the physical eye, except as manifesting through matter—but they are very real as all of us know by experience. You cannot see electricity, but when you receive its shock you realize its reality. You cannot see the force of gravity, but you become painfully aware of its reality when it drops an apple on your head; or causes you to fall suddenly when you make a misstep on the curb of the street. In fact, it is realized by all advanced occultists, that if there really can be said to be any degrees in reality between things, the balance is in favor of the finer forms of substance and forces, and against the less fine.

So, student, never permit yourself to think of the Astral as something comparatively unreal, or as only relatively existent. I, of course, am not speaking of Reality in the metaphysical sense of the term, for in such sense the entire manifested universe, including all of its planes, is unreal as compared to the One Reality. And, again, do not permit yourself to think of the astral senses as being one whit less real, reliable and important than those of the physical body. Each class of sense perception has its own proper field in which it is king. Each is master in its own realm. And there should be no attempt to draw distinctions of reality between them. At the last, they are all but the mechanism of consciousness, or "awareness," each adapted to the peculiar requirements of its environment.

The Astral has its scenery, geography (!), and "things," just as has the material world. These things are just as real as are England, the Vatican, St. Paul's, the Capitol at Washington; Broadway, Picadilly, or the Rue de la Paix; the Great Redwood Trees of California, the Grand Canyon, the Alps, or the Black Forest. Its inhabitants are just as real as any of the great men of the country in which you live, or those of any other country, whose names I hesitate to call, lest they pass from this material plane and thus become "unreal" even before these printed words pass before your eye, so impermanent are the inhabitants and things of even this real (!) material world.

The law of constant change operates on the Astral just as on the material plane. There, things come and go, just as they do here on the material plane. Stop a moment and concentrate on the gist of the matter, and you will see that the difference between the things of the two planes is simply like the difference between red and blue—simply a difference in the rate of vibration of substance. And, this again, is the cause of the difference between steel and hydrogen gas, between electricity and light, between magnetism and heat—simply a difference of vibrations of substance.

Moreover, and this is quite important to the student, the Astral has its laws just as has the material world. These laws must be learned and observed, otherwise the inhabitants of the Astral, as well as the visitor thereto, will reap the result which always comes from broken natural laws.

Again, there exists what may be called the "geography" of the Astral, if this material-plane word is permitted in this connection. There are regions, points of space, places, kingdoms, countries, etc., on the Astral, just as on the material plane. Sometimes these Astral regions have no connection with any on the material plane, while in other cases they have a very direct connection with and relation to, material places and the inhabitants thereof.

One may travel from one region of the Astral to another, by simply an act of will which raises the vibration of the astral body, without it moving a point in space. Again, one may travel in space from one point to another on the Astral, in cases where these points have some relation to points on the material plane.

As an instance of this latter form of travel, I would say that one may travel in the Astral from Berlin to Bombay—in but the twinkle of an eye, as regards time,—by merely wishing or willing to do so. Yes! time and space have their manifestation on the Astral. But, nevertheless, certain Astral manifestations, on its seven-times-seven sub-planes, may be, and likely are, present THERE in, at, and on, the exact point of space which you are occupying at this moment on the material plane—and this very moment of time, NOW!

If you have the knowledge and power, you, without leaving your seat, may traverse all of these sub-planes, one after the other, witnessing their scenery and inhabitants, their phenomena and activity, and then return to the material plane—all in a moment of time, and without changing a single point in space.

Or, if you prefer, you may travel to any of these sub-planes of the Astral, at your point of space, and then travel in space on the Astral to some other place on that sub-plane; and then have the choice of returning either the same way by which you came, or else descending to the material plane and travelling on it, in your astral body, back to where your physical body is resting. Read over these last two paragraphs, until you get the idea clearly fixed in your mind, for by so doing you will be able to comprehend more easily that which I shall have to say to you in the following chapters of this book.

In travelling on the Astral, one meets with many strange inhabitants of that wonderful realm of Nature—some pleasant and others unpleasant. Some of these inhabitants have passed on from the material plane, while others have never dwelt there, these latter forms being natives of the Astral and peculiar to itself.

In my personal class instruction, I have found it advantageous to my students for me to describe the phenomena of the Astral to them in my lectures, in the form of the story of a trip in the Astral, rather than as a dry, technical description. In such lectures, I assume that the students are present on the Astral with me, and that I am acting as their guide. In this way, a much clearer conception of the subject seems to be gained by them. After careful consideration, I have decided to follow this same plan—in part, at least—in some of the following chapters. I need scarcely add that the descriptions given are based upon the actual experiences of advanced occultists, including myself, and are not dogmatic statements of theory, conjectures, or speculations of mere "book occultists." Every fact herein stated may be verified by the experience of any advanced occultist.

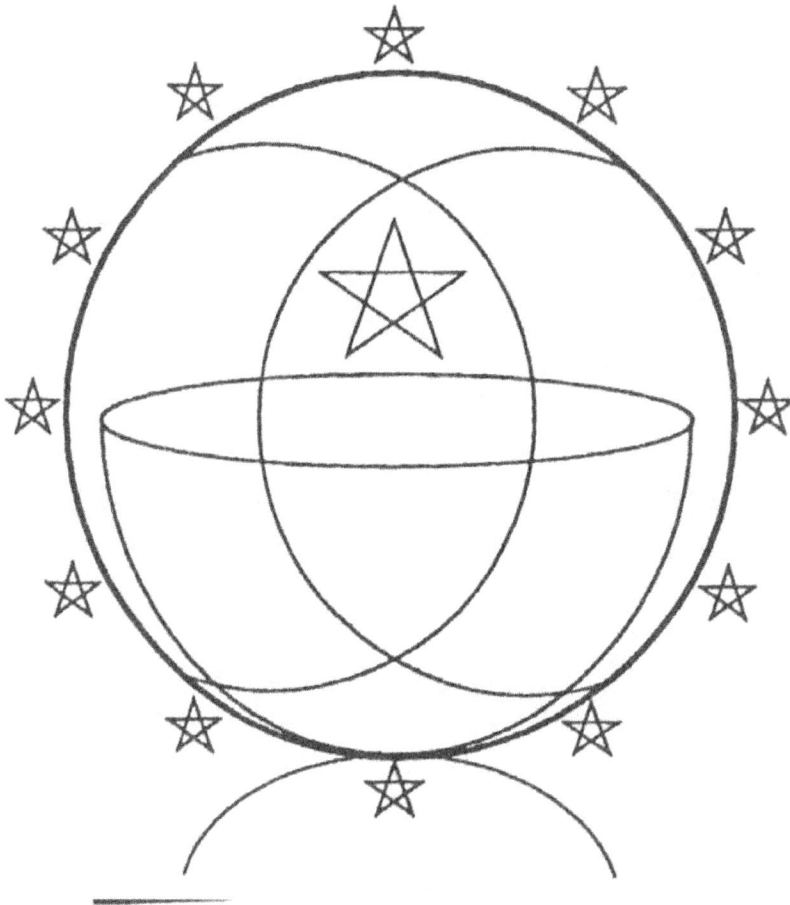

CHAPTER IV.

PASSING THE BORDER.

I DO not deem it advisable to enter into a description of the technical details attend-ant upon the process of passing out of the physical body into the astral body of finer substance. Any description of this kind, even though it be but merely a suggestion of the facts, might give an untrained person at least a hint of the process, which might lead him to experiment, and which might bring upon him very undesirable results. I shall pass over this stage, for the reasons stated, which will meet with the approval of every advanced occultist and careful student of occultism. * * *

Now, student, you find yourself outside of your physical form or body, and clad in your astral form alone. You probably think that I am joking with you, for as you glance at your body you find that it appears not different from your ordinary one. Even your clothing is the same, to the most minute detail—this occurs through perfectly natural laws on the Astral plane, which I cannot take time to explain at this time.

You realize, however, that you are indeed

out of the physical body, when you turn your head and perceive your own physical form, as well as mine, seemingly sunk in sleep in the arm chairs in which we seated ourselves a few moments ago.

Looking a little closer, you will see that your astral form, as well as mine, is connected with its physical counterpart by a tiny, thin, tenuous filament of ethereal substance, resembling a rope of shining spider-web silk. This filament is capable of expansion, and contraction, and enables you to move about freely.

Now concentrate your attention as you have been taught to do, and will that your vibrations increase in rate, but in perfect harmony with mine, so that you will keep in my company instead of moving on to other sub-planes or sub-visions, parting with my company. You would not find it exactly safe or pleasant to leave my presence, until you have learned to pilot yourself in these strange waters.

You will find yourself with me in a strange atmosphere, although you have not moved an inch in space. Behind you, so to speak, you perceive dimly the room in which we were just living; and ahead of you, so to speak, you perceive strange flashes and streaks of phosphorescent light of different hues and tints.

These are the vibrations and waves of force, for you are now passing through the Plane of Forces. That vivid, bluish streak is the passage of some electric current—probably a wireless message flashing through space. Back of you, on my table, you see the magnetic ore, or lodestone, paper-weight, which always lies there. But now you see the peculiar phosphorescence around its poles, which is not visible on the material plane.

You also notice a peculiar faint vibratory glow around every physical object—this is the force of atomic and molecular attraction, etc. Still fainter, you find a peculiar radiance permeating the entire atmosphere—this is the outward sign of the force of gravitation. These things are all very interesting, and if you were a learned physicist, or great physical scientist, you could scarcely be dragged from this plane, so interesting would be the study of force made visible. But, as you are not such a person, you will see more interesting sights ahead of you.

Now, you feel your life force vibrating at a higher rate, and realize that the sense of weight seems to be dropping from you. You feel as light as a feather, and feel as though you could move without an effort. Well, you may begin to walk. Yes, "walk," I said! You are still on earth, and the floor of the room is still there under your feet.

Let us walk through the wall of the room, and out into the street. Don't be afraid, step through the wall as if it were made of fog. There, you see how easy it is. Odd thing, really stepping through a brick and stone wall, isn't it? But it's still more odd when you stop to consider that as we moved the wall really passed through our thin substance, instead of the latter passing through the wall—that's the real secret of it.

Now let us walk down the street. Step out just as if you were in the flesh—stop a moment! there you let that man walk right through you! And he never even saw you! Do you realize that we are ghosts? Just as much a ghost as was Hamlet's father, except that his physical body was mouldering in the ground, while ours are asleep awaiting our return to them. There! that dog saw you. And that horse vaguely feels your presence! See how nervous he is! Animals possess very keen psychic senses, compared to those of man.

But cease thinking of yourself, and look closely at the persons passing by you. You notice that each one is surrounded by an egg-

shaped aura extending on all sides of him to
the distance of about two or three feet. Do
you notice the kaleidoscopic play of blending
colors in the aura? Notice the difference in
the shades and tints of these colors, and also
observe the predominance of special colors in
each case! You know what these colors mean,
for I have instructed you regarding them in my
teaching on "The Human Aura, and Astral
Colors."

Notice that beautiful spiritual blue around
that woman's head! And see that ugly muddy
red around that man passing her! Here comes
an intellectual giant—see that beautiful golden
yellow around his head, like a nimbus! But I
don't exactly like that shade of red around his
body—and there is too marked an absence of
blue in his aura! He lacks harmonious development.

Do you notice those great clouds of semi-
luminous substance, which are slowly floating
along?—notice how the colors vary in them.
Those are clouds of thought vibrations, repre-
senting the composite thought of a multitude
of people. Also notice how each body of
thought is drawing to itself little fragments of
similar thought forms and energy. You see
here the tendency of thought forces to attract

others of their kind—how like the proverbial birds of a feather, they flock together—how thoughts come home, bringing their friends with them—how each man creates his own thought atmosphere.

Speaking of atmospheres, do you notice that each shop we pass has its own peculiar thought atmosphere? If you look into the houses on either side of the street, you will see that the same thing is true. The very street itself has its own atmosphere, created by the composite thought of those inhabiting and frequenting it. No! do not pass down that side street—its astral atmosphere is too depressing, and its colors too horrible and disgusting for you to witness just now—you might get discouraged and fly back to your physical body for relief!

Look at those thought forms flying through the atmosphere! What a variety of form and coloring! Some most beautiful, the majority quite neutral in tint, and occasionally a fierce, fiery one tearing its way along toward its mark. Observe those whirling and swirling tiny cyclonic thought-forms as they are thrown off from that business house. Across the street, notice that great octopus monster of a thought-form, with its great tentacles striving to wind around passing persons and draw them into that flashy dance-hall and dram-shop. A devilish monster which we would do well to destroy. Turn your concentrated thought upon it, and will it out of existence—there, that's the right way; watch it sicken and shrivel! But alas! more of its kind will come forth from that place.

Here, will yourself up above the level of the housetops—you can do it easily, if you only realize that you can—there, I have helped you to do it this time, it's quite easy when you once gain confidence. However, if you lose confidence, and grow afraid, down you will tumble to the ground, and will bruise your astral body.

From this height look down around you. You will see a great multitude of tiny candle-like lights—each represents a human soul. Here or there you will see a few much brighter lights, and far apart you will see some that shine like a brilliant electric spark—these last are the auric symbols of an advanced soul. "Let your light so shine—"! Behold the radiance emerging from that humble house of religious worship, and contrast it with the unpleasant auric atmosphere of that magnificent church structure next door to it—can you not read the story of spirituality and the lack of it in the cases of these churches?

But these sights, interesting though they be, and as useful as they are in illustrating the lessons you have learned in the class, or from the manual, are far less in the scale than those which we shall witness in a moment. Come, take my hand. Our vibrations are raising. * * * Come!

CHAPTER V.

SOME LOWER SUB-PLANES.

NOW, student, we are entering the vibrations of the lower sub-planes of the Astral. You must nerve yourself to witness some unpleasant sights, but be not afraid for nothing can harm you here while I am with you. Were you alone here, lacking the knowledge of self-protection, you might find the experience very terrifying. But, even then, though you lacked the higher knowledge, if you would but maintain a positive mental state, and deny the power of the Astral inhabitants to harm you, you would still be safe. A firm mental attitude, and the assertion of your own immunity will act as a barrier through which these influences cannot penetrate.

Your first impression is that the material world is still around you, with all its scenes plainly visible. But, as you look you will find that there seems to be a peculiar veil between those scenes and the plane upon which you are temporarily dwelling. This veil, while at least semi-transparent, nevertheless seems to have a peculiar appearance of resistent solidity and you find yourself instinctively realizing that it would be a barrier to the passage of the astral entities back to the material plane.

I now change our vibrations, for a moment, to those of a very unpleasant subdivision of the lowest sub-plane. This is the subdivision which the old occultists were wont to call "the Astral cemetery." We shall stay on this plane of vibrations but for a moment, for it furnishes a ghastly sight, and its atmosphere is most depressing. Now, hold tight to me, and press close up to me, for you will instinctively feel the need of protection. Gazing around you on all sides, you will see what appear to be the disintegrating forms of human beings, and even some animals. These forms seem to be floating in space. They seem real, and yet, some way, not real. You realize that they are not physical bodies, but still they bear too close a resemblance to physical corpses to be pleasant. Take one good look around you, for I shall change our vibrations in a moment. * * * There! we have left that scene behind us! But before proceeding further, we shall pause a moment and consider what we have just witnessed.

These disintegrating astral forms are what occultists know as the "astral shells." The astral shell is really an astral corpse, just as the physical body in the grave is the material corpse. For, as we shall presently see, the disembodied soul eventually leaves the Astral and moves on to what the occultists know as the mental or spiritual planes of being, which are symbolized by the race conception of "the heavens," of which all religions teach. When the soul so passes on, it leaves behind it the astral body it has inhabited while on the Astral. This astral body, or form, then begins to disintegrate, and in time disappears altogether, being resolved to its original elements. During this process, it dwells on this particular division of one of the lower subdivisions of the lowest Astral sub-plane. This particular division has no other purpose, and is separate and apart from the other subdivisions.

There is a great difference between the astral shells of different individuals, so far as is concerned the duration of the shells in this particular place of disintegration. For instance, the astral of a person of high spirituality and ideals will disintegrate very rapidly indeed, as its atoms have little or no cohesive attraction when once it is discarded. But, on the other hand, the astral shell of a person of earthly ideals and material tendencies will hold

together for a comparatively long time, so
strong is the attractive force generated while
the shell is occupied by its owner.

Those astral bodies are "dead" and have no
consciousness or intelligence, and as a rule cannot even be galvanized into appearing a life
as can the class of astral forms known as the
"spectres," or "shades," which belong to a
slightly different category, and which we shall
now glance at for a moment. * * * There!
gaze on the scene for a moment, before I
change the vibrations again. * * *

Our momentary glimpse of the subdivision
of the Astral upon which the spectral forms
abide, was not a pleasant one, but it is interesting because it explains some peculiar features
of psychic or occult phenomena which is often
misinterpreted. You noticed that instead of
floating about in astral space, as did the shells
which we saw a few moments back, these
spectres acted like shadowy human beings in
a dazed or dreamlike condition. You saw them
walking dreamily about, without set object or
purpose—a weird, unpleasant sight.

These spectres are really astral shells from
which the souls have departed, but which have
left in them sufficient power, arising from the
former thought and will vibrations of their

owners, to give them a temporary semblance of life and action. This power gradually wears away, and the shell then sinks to the subdivision which we saw a little further back. In the meantime, it dwells on this particular subdivision.

In the case of the soul with high ideals and spiritual aspirations, there are practically no material thought vibrations remaining to "galvanize" the astral body after the soul has withdrawn itself. Its higher nature has neutralized these lower, but strong, vibrations. But in the case of the soul retaining strong material thoughts and desires, the power is much stronger. In the latter class, even after the higher nature of the soul has drawn it upward, above the Astral, these lower mental vibrations may persist in the deserted astral form, and thus give to the latter a semblance of life and activity which, though a counterfeit, may manifest considerable power for a time.

The counterfeit power of these spectral forms steadily decreases, but in some cases it persists for a comparatively long time. As a rule, the power disappears in the way stated, but in certain other cases it is used up, as a spark is rendered bright by blowing upon it, by means of a psychic stimulus from persons living on the material plane. I am now alluding to the power generated in "circles," and through mediumistic persons, on the material plane or earth life. The psychic power so generated, coupled with the strong mental attraction set up between persons in earth life and the spectral form, may cause the latter to manifest itself to the former, either by more or less complete materialization, or by partial manifestation through the physical organism of the medium, or mediums, present.

In such a case, the spectre, reanimated and "galvanized" into seeming life by means of the psychic power of the medium, or those composing the psychic circle, will strive to manifest itself by speech, automatic writing, raps, or otherwise. But, at the best, its efforts will be feeble and faulty, and the persons witnessing the phenomena will always remember the same with the dim idea that "there was something wrong about it"—something was found to be lacking. In some cases, the vibration of old memories will survive in the spectral form, which will enable it to answer questions fairly well, and to allude to past experiences. But even then, in these cases there will be a shadow of unreality which will impress the careful observer.

Remember, there are many other forms of "spirit return," partial or complete, but much that passes for the real phenomena is really but a manifestation of the presence of these spectral forms of whose real nature we have been made acquainted by our glimpse into their region of abode. Moreover, these entities (if they may be called by that name) borrow ideas and impressions from the minds of the mediums or persons in the circle, in addition to their own shadowy memories, and thus doubly become reflections or counterfeits.

These spectres have really no soul. The soul which formerly occupied the form has departed to a higher plane, and is in ignorance of the performance of its discarded shell. It is pathetic to witness cases where these counterfeit spectral form are accepted as the departed soul of the individual, by those who loved him in earth life. A lack of knowledge of true occultism often permits of deplorable mistakes of this kind. The true occultist is never deceived in this manner. These spectres are no more "departed souls" or "spirits" than a galvanized physical corpse is the individual which once inhabited it, though the current may cause it to move its muscles and go through the motions of life. It remains a corpse and discarded shell—and that is just what the spectral form is, plus the remaining vibratory echoes of its old mental life.

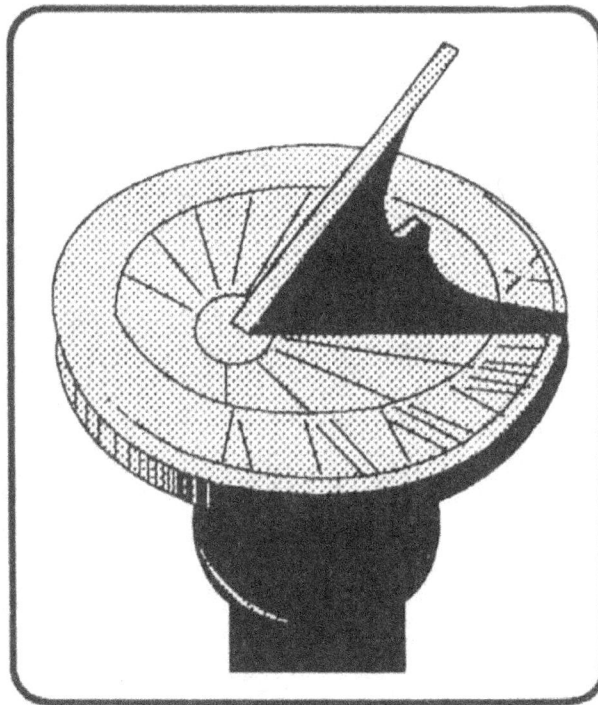

CHAPTER VI.

DISEMBODIED SOULS.

YOU very naturally inquire: "But where are the disembodied souls, themselves? I expected to see them as soon as we crossed the border of the Astral!" Yes! that is the general expectation of the neophyte in occultism, when he gets his first glimpse into the Astral scenes. But, unless he happens to stumble at once upon certain sub-planes, he is apt to be disappointed. But, the better way is to let you learn the story by viewing the various sub-planes, at the same time listening to my explanation of that which you witness on them.

You will notice that our vibrations are now changing, and growing more intense. We are now entering upon a very wonderful sub-plane, or rather, upon one of the subdivisions of such a plane. This region, I ask you to remember, is one the entry to which is strictly guarded by the law of the Astral, and watched over by certain very high spiritual influences. It is a sacred place. No one is admitted here as a visitor, unless he be of high spirituality and pure heart. Even a trained occultist, unless he possess these qualifications, finds it impossible to enter these vibrations.

This region is the resting place of the disembodied souls for some time after they have left the physical body. In it they dwell in peaceful slumber, until Nature performs certain work in preparing them for their new plane of life. This stage has been compared to the cocoon-stage, between the stage of the caterpillar and that of the butterfly, in which stage a complete transformation is effected, and the wings of the new life are developed to take the place of the old crawling form.

We are now on this particular sub-plane. Enter upon a contemplation of its wonders, with all reverence and love of all mankind. On all sides, stretching away as far as the eye can see, you perceive the slumbering forms of disembodied souls, each astral form resting in dreamless sleep. And, yet, even if you were not so informed, you would recognize that these forms are not dead, but are merely sleeping. There is none of the atmosphere of death or corpses about this region. Nothing depressing, you notice. Nothing but a sense of infinite calm and peace. Being spiritually developed yourself, you doubtless feel the presence of certain great spiritual entities—though you see them not, because their vibrations are too high for you to see them even by astral vision—these are the great spiritual guardians of this realm, who protect the slumber of the souls at rest herein—the Great Watchers of the Sleeping Souls.

If you will watch carefully, you will notice here and there a movement indicating the awakening of some of these resting forms. A moment later the form disappears from the scene—it seemingly melts into nothingness. But it still is existent—its vibrations simply have changed, and it has moved on to another sub-plane, or division thereof, without having been aware of the scenes of this place. It has begun its real life after death. Let us move on, leaving this scene behind us, while I explain to you some of the phenomena of this period of existence of the disembodied soul. * * * Let us pause here, on the quiet sub-plane, until the matter is made plain to you.

It is a common teaching of many religions that the disembodied soul enters at once upon its heaven or hell. The Roman Catholic Church, and some branches of Buddhism, however, teach of an intermediate state called Purgatory, or a similar name. Some denominations of the Christian Church hold that all

souls slumber in unconsciousness, until the
call of the great trumpet of Judgment Day,
when all awaken from their long sleep and are
judged and sent to the place of reward or
punishment, as their cases may deserve. You
see on the Astral some things which show
you that all of these views have a basis in
fact, and yet how imperfect are these conceptions of the theologies!

All occultists know, however, that nearly all
of the original religious teachers had a very
complete knowledge of the real facts of the
Astral, and higher planes, and merely handed
down to their followers such fragments of the
truth as they thought could be assimilated at
the time. All of the theological teachings
regarding the Life after Death—heavens and
hells—contain some truth, but none contain all
the truth.

In the majority of cases, the mind of the
dying person sinks into the slumber of
so-called death, and awakens only after a
period of restful, transforming slumber upon
the Astral, in the region we have just seen.
In some cases, however, there is a brief wak-
ing, like a semi-awakening from a dream,
shortly after the departure from the physical
body, in which case the astral body may

appear, visibly, to some friend, associate or
loved one—or even in the scenes in which the
person usually spent much of his time, as, for
instance, his office, shop, study, etc.   This
accounts for the occasional instances of the
disembodied person so appearing, of which
there are many well authenticated cases.   But
even in such event, the disembodied soul soon
becomes drowsy, and sinks into the pre-
liminary sleep of the Astral, moving on to the
region we have just left.

There is a great difference in the time in
which the disembodied soul slumbers in this
state.   Strange and paradoxical as it may
appear, the highest and lowest souls in the
scale of development, awaken first.   The average soul slumbers far longer than either.   I
will explain the reason of this to you in a
moment.

The highly spiritual person, needing but
comparatively little transformation to fit him
for the higher planes, may slumber here only
a very short time, and then passes on to some
of the higher astral planes; or, in cases of high
development, may omit these higher astral
planes, and pass on at once to the plane or
planes above the Astral—into what occultists
know as the "heavens," which, technically, are

regions of the mental plane, and the ones still higher. The average soul, however, slumbers a much longer time, many years, perhaps, and then awakens upon a higher astral plane suited to its requirements.

The low, material soul, as a rule, awakens very speedily, and passes at once to the low plane for which it has an affinity. But, note this difference: the highly developed soul awakens speedily, for the reason that it has less to slough off and be transformed into higher attributes—the work is already partially performed.

The average soul, on the other hand, requires a much greater transformation for its scenes of higher activities, and so remains much longer in the transforming sleep; and, last (note the seeming paradox, and its explanation), the low, material soul awakens speedily, not because it has been transformed easily for the higher scenes, but, on the contrary, because it is not destined for these higher scenes— it never reaches them, but descends to a low plane of the Astral, where it lives out its low inclinations and ideals, until it finally sickens of them, at least to an extent, and then is ready for further transformation.

All souls, however, high or low, eventually

move off the Astral and enter into the place, or rather the state, of the Mental Plane, or the regions of the "heavens," leaving their astral shells behind them. Some of the highest, as I have said, mount to these planes without any intervening stay on the higher Astral, but the majority have their share of Astral life, higher and lower.

On the "heaven" planes, the spiritual souls spend great periods of time enjoying the well-earned bliss. Souls lower in development spend less time there. The low, material souls, scarcely taste the experience of those high regions. I shall speak further regarding this, as we proceed.

As a general rule, I would remind you, the higher the advancement of a soul, the greater the time between its incarnations; and vice versa. There are special cases, however, such as the call to duty on the part of a high soul, or a strong attraction to another, or others, approaching reincarnation, which may bring back a high soul in a shorter time than it really deserves—this is simply renunciation, however, on the part of the high soul, and is not a violation of the general rule as stated a moment ago.

Let us now change our vibrations, and visit

some of the scenes of Astral life, in which the awakened souls are living, moving, and having their being. A few actual illustrations of life on these planes will teach you more regarding this great subject, than would volumes of books, or years of verbal teaching. Let us begin at some of the lowest sub-planes, and their divisions—the sight is not pleasant, but you will gain a valuable lesson. * * *

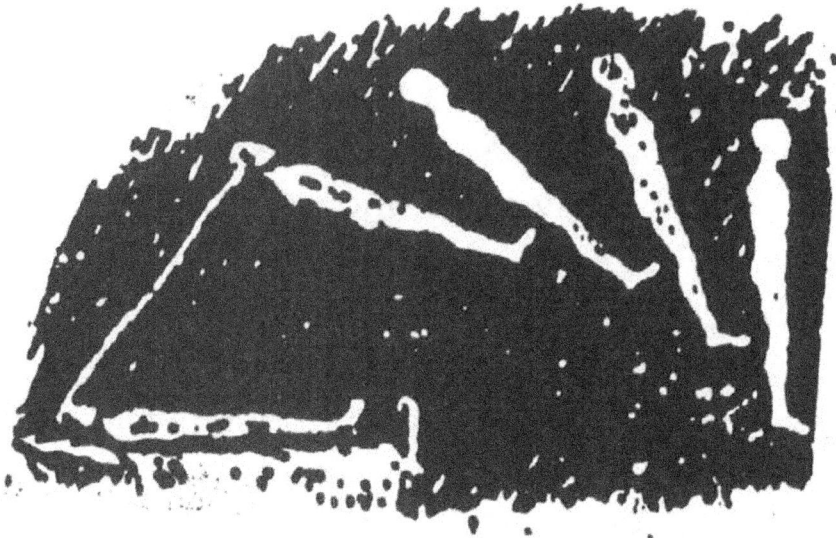

CHAPTER VII.

SCENES OF THE ASTRAL.

WE are now vibrating on a very low subdivision of the lowest sub-plane of the Astral. You are conscious of a very unpleasant feeling, and an almost physical repulsion to the atmosphere around you. Some very sensitive natures experience a feeling of being surrounded by a dense, sticky, foul, foggy atmosphere, through which they must almost force their way, when they visit these regions. It is akin to the feelings experienced by a high-minded spiritual person on the earth plane, if he happens to enter a place inhabited by persons of a lewd, vulgar, depraved nature and character—this magnified many degrees by reason of the astral laws.

It is no wonder that one of the old Egyptian writers, whose work survives on graven stone, said, some four thousand years ago: "What manner of foul region is this into which I have foolishly come? It is without water; without air; it is unfathomably deep; it has the darkness of the blackest night, when the sky is overcast with dense clouds, and no ray of light penetrates their curtain. Souls wander hopelessly and helplessly about herein; in it there is no peace, no calm, no rest, no quiet of the heart or mind. It is an abomination and desolation. Woe is the soul that abideth herein!"

Looking around you, in the dim, ghastly light of this region, you perceive countless human forms, of the most repulsive appearance. Some of them are so low in the scale as to seem almost beast-like, rather than human. There are still lower forms on the subdivisions just below this one, but I shall spare you the disgusting sight. These creatures are disembodied souls, in the astral body, living on the low plane to which they descended when awakening from their very brief astral sleep.

If you will peer through the enveloping fog, you will become conscious of the presence of the material world as a sort of background. To you it appears detached, and removed in space, but to these creatures—these low souls—the two planes seem to be blended. To them, they appear actually to be abiding in the scenes and among the persons of the lowest phases of earth life. Even you find that you can see only the very low earth-scenes in the background—the higher scenes appear blotted out with great smears, like a censored newspaper page in war times. To these poor souls there is no earth world except these scenes which accord with their old desires.

But while apparently living amid these old familiar and congenial low earth-scenes, these souls are really suffering the fate of Tantalus. For while they plainly see these scenes, and all that is going on in them, they cannot otherwise participate in the revels and debaucheries which they perceive plainly—they can SEE only—as for the rest they participate only vicariously. This renders the place a veritable hell for them, for they are constantly tantalized and tormented by sights of scenes in which they cannot participate. They can exercise simply "the lust of the eye," which is but as a thorn in the flesh to them. On all sides, on earth-life, they see their kind (in the flesh) eating, drinking, gambling, engaging in all forms of debauchery and brutality—and while they eagerly cluster around, they cannot make their presence felt (under ordinary circumstances) nor can they participate in the scenes which they witness. The lack of the physical body is indeed a very hell to them, under such circumstances.

The astral atmosphere of low dram-shops, pool rooms, gambling hells, race tracks, "free-and-easies," brothels, "red-light" districts—and their more fashionable counterparts—are filled with these low astral forms of souls across the astral border. Occasionally, they are able to influence some earth companion, who is so saturated with liquor, or overcome by drugs, that he is physically open to such influences. When they so influence him, they strive to lead him into further degradation and debauchery, for, in so doing, they obtain a reflex-gratification, as it were. But I shall not dwell upon this subject—it is too loathsome.

In some instances, the sojourn on this low astral sub-plane sets up such a strong desire for rebirth in the flesh, among similar scenes, that the poor soul eagerly presses forward toward reincarnation on a similar low plane. In other cases, I am glad to say, the experience so sickens and disgusts the poor soul that it experiences a revulsion and disgust for such things, in which case the current of its desires naturally carries it in the opposite direction, and it is given the opportunity to rise in the scale of the Astral, where its better tendencies are encouraged, and a better rebirth finally results.

At the end, however, in nearly all cases

"living-out" results in "out-living," and even the lowest rises in time. Some few souls, however, sink so low as to be incapable of rising, and they meet the final fate (not of damnation) of annihilation. Even in these hells of the astral, however, the degraded souls are "punished not for their sins, but by them" as an old writer once forcibly stated it.

But this particular scene is not the only one on this sub-plane of the Astral—it has many counterparts. I cannot take time to show them all to you, or to describe them in detail. I can illustrate the idea, however, by stating that close to the scene you have just witnessed, is another in which the actors are those miserly, money-loving souls, who have sold all their better nature for the mess of pottage of worldly gain. The punishment, by the sin rather than for it, is similar to that of the low souls in the preceding scene. They are tormented by the sight, but are tantalized by not being able to participate. The result is practically similar to that mentioned in the last case—some find desire increased, and others find disgust and nausea and thus seek the way to higher things.

There are hundreds of similar regions on the lower Astral, some of which are much higher, however, than those we have just considered. All of them serve as a Purgatory, or place of the burning-out of desires of a low kind—not the burning of material flames, but by the fire of the desire itself, as we have seen. This idea of burning away, or purging, of the low desires, is found to permeate nearly all religions, and has its basis in the facts of the Astral.

Changing our vibrations, and mounting to higher sub-planes, we pass rapidly from scene to scene. You appear astonished to notice that many of these scenes seem to be set to scenery, like a great theatre. You notice with wonder the artificial nature of this astral scenery, and wonder at the fact that the people on these scenes seem to regard this scenery as natural and real, instead of make-believe. It all seems very shadowy and imperfect to you, but very real to them. The secret is that the scenery is the creation of the minds of those taking part in the scenes, and those who have preceded them on this plane. It is all make-believe—a mirage, so to speak—but very real to those taking part in the scenes.

It is not the purpose of this little book to describe the chemistry of the Astral by means of which it is possible for the mind to build up scenery, etc., from the astral substance. To the advanced occultist, who has studied deeply the occult chemistry, the matter is as simple as is the formation of ice from water, which in turn was once steam—and at the same time as wonderful. The traveller on the Astral always will bear witness to the wonders of that plane, the scenery of which is all built up in this way, though he may not be able to explain the chemistry of its formation.

In this way, on the various higher planes of the Astral, including some of the comparatively lower planes, we find beautiful mountains and valleys, rivers and lakes, cities, towns, villages and country-land—in fact, all forms of scenery known in earth life. We also see buildings of all kinds, and all varieties of household utensils, implements, furniture, etc. All are built from the astral substance by means of the imaginative minds of the dwellers on those planes. To the visitor they seem most unreal—one can actually see through them, and on all sides of them at one time, as in the case of a transparent crystal. But to the dwellers on the Astral they are as solid and real as are their material counterparts— and no doubt regarding their solidity ever enters the mind of the Astral inhabitant.

And what is the purpose of all this theatrical make-believe of the Astral? you well ask. You will see in a moment, when I give you the key that unlocks the secret doors of the Astral life and its meaning.

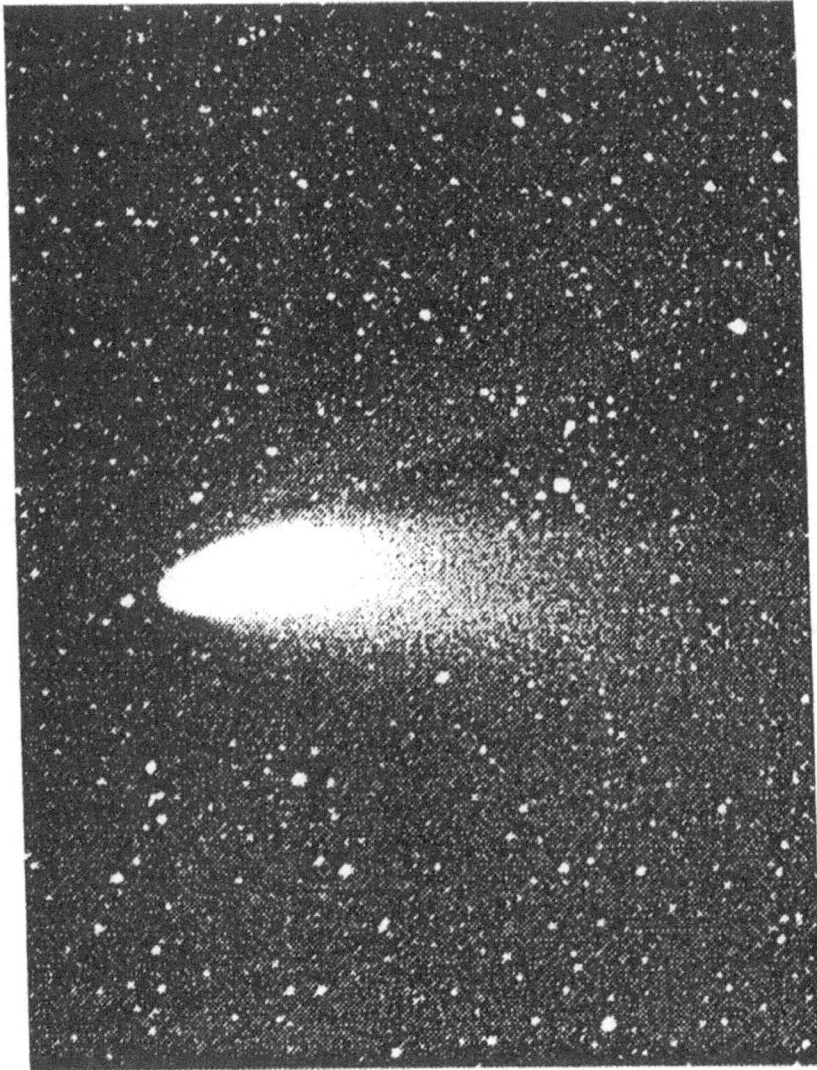

CHAPTER VIII.

LIFE AND WORK ON THE ASTRAL.

WHAT I have just said regarding the nature of the astral scenery must not be taken as indicating that the Astral, itself, is merely imaginary or unreal in any sense. Nor is the substance of which the scenery is composed any less real than the substance of which the material world is composed. On the material plane, substance manifests as matter; while on the astral plane it manifests in a finer form of "stuff" or material. Again, on the material plane, the material, or matter, is shaped by the physical forces of nature, or, perhaps, by the mind of man using the original material in order to build "artificial" structures or forms.

On the Astral, on the other hand, the astral material is not thrown into shape by physical forces, but is shaped and formed only by the thought and imaginative power of the minds of those inhabiting that plane. But these shapes, forms and structures of the astral material are not to be thought of as existing merely in the mind of the astral dwellers. They have an independent existence of their own, being composed of astral material, though shaped, formed and built up directly by the mind-power of the astral dwellers, instead of by the physical forces of nature.

The astral scenery, etc., survives the passing away of the mind which built it up, and disintegrates only after the passage of considerable time, just as do the material things on the earth plane. As for the power of the imagination of man, do not be deceived for a moment—for this is one of the most efficient powers in nature, and operates strongly even on the material plane, though on the Astral its power is more easily recognized by the senses. To the dwellers on the Astral, their scenery, buildings, etc., are as solid as are those of the material plane to the dwellers thereupon.

Passing through the various sub-planes, and their divisions, on the Astral you notice a great variety of scenery, and a great difference in the character and occupations of the inhabitants. But, you notice one general characteristic underlying all of the differences, namely, the fact that all of these persons (astral dwellers) seem to be filled with an intense earnestness, and manifest a degree of concentration which gives to them an appearance of being preoccupied. This, often, to such an extent that they seem to be oblivious to our presence and passage through their midst, unless we address them directly. Again, everyone seems to be busy, even when their tasks are those of sport or play.

The key to the occupation and pursuits of the dwellers on the Astral is found in the principle that the life of the soul on the comparatively higher divisions of the Astral consists in a working out of the intellectual desires, and ordinary tendencies, tastes, likes, and aspirations which they were unable to manifest fully in earth life. I do not mean the low sensual desires, or purely animal tastes, but rather the "ambitions" and similar forms of desire or strong inclinations. Many of these inclinations may be very creditable and praiseworthy, rather than otherwise, but they are all concerned with physical manifestations, rather than with spiritual unfoldment and evolution in the strict sense of these terms. The higher planes are those in which the spiritual forces bud and flower, and bear fruit—the Astral, even on its highest planes, is the scene of the living-out, and working-out, of earthly intellectual and similar ambitions and aspirations.

The higher the plane of the Astral world, the less are the old earth scenes in evidence, even in the shape of the dim background we saw as we progressed on our journey. As we mounted on the scale, these old earth scenes grew very dim, and where we are standing now, on the fourth sub-plane, they are practically out of sight. This particular sub-plane is not particularly elevating, but nevertheless is interesting to the student.

As we pass from scene to scene, we see the "happy hunting grounds" of the American Indians, thickly settled with these old aborigines who have been dwelling there for quite a period of time. They are busy, and happy hunting their astral buffaloes, and other game (all artificially created by their imagination, from the astral substance, and having no real existence as living, feeling animals). A little further on, we witness similar forms of the "Spirit-land" of other primitive people, in some of which the disembodied warriors fight and conquer great hosts of artificial foes, and then have great feasts according to their old customs.

Valhalla is here, as well as the other imaginary Paradises of the old races of men. But their inhabitants are dwindling in number, being caught up in the current bearing them on to reincarnation. But, note this, that while there is nothing elevating in the pursuits followed in these scenes, there is nothing degrading or lowering, from a strictly spiritual point of view. But, there is in evidence always a living-out, and wearing-out, of the old desires of this kind, to make room for higher ones— all tends toward spiritual evolution.

Raising our vibrations rapidly, and passing over many degrees of scenes of this kind, we find ourselves on a considerably higher plane. Here we see men engaged in what would be called "useful work" in earth life. But they are performing it not as labor, but rather as a joyous recreation. Observing closely, you will see that the work is all of an inventive and constructive nature. The men and women are perfecting that in which their interest was engaged while on earth life. They are improving on their work, and are filled with the joy of creation. They remind one forcibly of Kipling's mention of the future state when: " . . . no one shall work for money, and no one shall work for fame; but each for the joy of the working." On some of these subdivisions we see the artist busily at work, turning out wonderful masterpieces; also musicians creating great compositions, of which they had vainly dreamt while in earth-life. The architect builds great structures—the inventor discovers great things. And all are filled with the joy of work, and the ecstacy of creative imagination.

But, make not the mistake, student, of regarding this as merely play, or as possibly a form of reward for well-done world work, though, of course, both of these elements play their part in the general working of the Law. The main thing to remember is that in this work on the Astral, there is an actual mental advance and progress.

Moreover, in many cases, here on these very planes of the Astral there is being built the mould from which will actually pour great inventive and creative achievements, on the material plane, in the future incarnations of these souls now doing work on this plane. The Astral is the great pattern shop of the world. Its patterns are reproduced in matter when the soul revisits the earth scenes. Many a work of art, musical composition, great piece of literature, or great invention, has been but a reproduction of an Astral pattern. This will help to explain the feeling common to all great performers of creative, imaginative or intellectual work—the strange feeling that their work is but a completion of something at which they had previously wrought—a re-discovery, as it were.

Again, in this work-play of the Astral, the soul is always at work using up old ideas, aspirations, etc., and discarding them finally. In this way real progress is made, for after all even earth-life is seen to be largely a matter of "living-out and out-living"—of mounting higher on the steps of each mistake and each failure. In the work of the Astral many old ideas are worked out and discarded; many old longings exhausted and discarded; many old ambitions manifested and then left behind on the trail. There is a certain "burning up, and burning out" of old mental material, and a place made for new and better material in the new earth life. Often, in this way, on the Astral there is accomplished as much in the direction of improvement and progress, as would be possible only in quite a number of earth-lives. Life on the Astral is very earnest and intense—the vibrations are much higher than on the material plane.

Bearing this principle in mind, these Astral scenes which you are now witnessing take on a great and new meaning. You recognize them as very important school-rooms in the great school of life. Work is being done here that can not be accomplished elsewhere. Everything has its meaning. There is no waste effort, or useless activity in the universe, no matter what the careless observer may say to the contrary. The Astral is no joke of the universe—it is one of its great, real workshops and laboratories of the soul. It has its distinct place in the work of spiritual unfoldment and evolution.

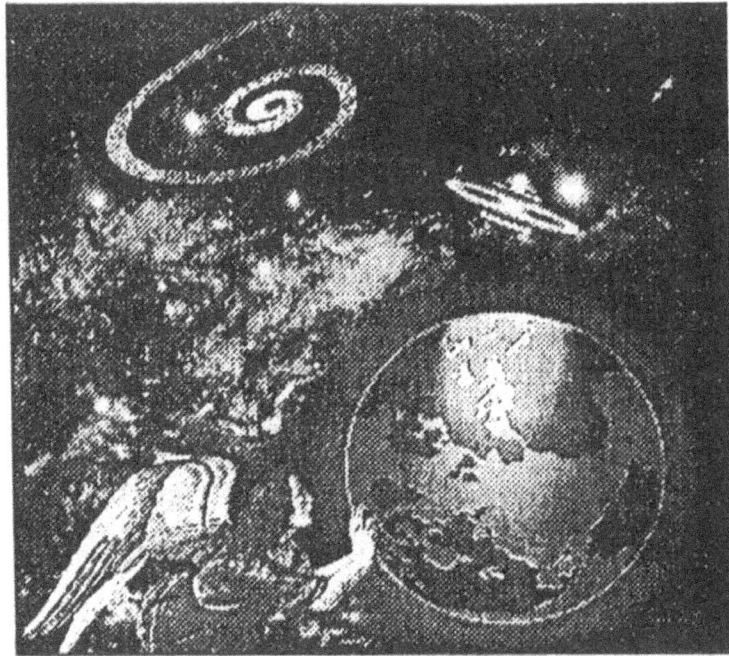

CHAPTER IX.

HIGHER PLANES AND BEYOND.

RAISING our vibrations a little, we now enter upon the great second sub-plane of the Astral, with its seven subdivisions and its many minor divisions and regions. Almost before I tell you, you will feel the religious atmosphere pervading this region. For this is the plane upon which the religious aspirations and emotions find full power of expression. On this sub-plane are many souls who have spent some time on the other sub-planes of the Astral, doing their work there and then passing on to these scenes in order to manifest this part of their natures.

But, I wish to call your attention to the occult distinction between "spirituality" and "religion." Spirituality is the recognition of the divine spark within the soul, and the unfoldment of the same into consciousness; while religion, in the occult sense, consists of observance of certain forms of worship, rites, ceremonies, etc., the holding to certain forms of theology, and the manifestation of what may be called the religious emotions. The religious instinct is deeply implanted in the hearts of men, and may be called the stepping-stone toward true spirituality—but it is not spirituality itself. In its higher forms, it is a beautiful thing, but in its lower ones it leads to narrowness and bigotry—but it is a necessary step on the Path, and all must mount it in order to reach higher things.

This second sub-plane of the Astral is filled with a multitude of souls each of whom is endeavoring to manifest and express his own particular shade of religious conception. It may be said to contain all the heavens that have ever been dreamed of in theology, and taught in the churches—each filled with devotees of the various creeds. Each of the great religions has its own particular region, in which its disciples gather, worship, and rejoice. In each region the religious soul finds "just what he had expected" and hoped to find on "the other shore." Some remain content in their own place, while others growing dissatisfied drift toward some sub-region, or group, which comes nearer to their newly awakened conception of truth.

In passing rapidly through these regions, you will find that each has its own particular environment in exact accordance with the beliefs of the persons inhabiting it. Some have the appearance of a plain, old-fashioned meeting house, on an immense scale; while others resemble a gigantic cathedral, filled with gorgeous decorations and paraphernalia, and echoing with the sound of glorious litanies and other ritualistic forms of worship. Each has its officiating priests or preachers, according to its regulations. You see at a glance that the environment, scenery, buildings, decorations, etc., are built up from the astral substance by the imaginative power of the minds of those congregating at each point. All the stage-setting and properties are found fully in evidence (I say this in all seriousness, and with no attempt to be frivolous or flippant)—you may even see the golden crowns, harps, and stiff haloes, in some cases, and hear the sound of "the eternal chant of praise."

I regret to be compelled to call your attention to the regions of some lower forms of religion, in which there is a background picture of a burning hell, at which the devotees gaze with satisfaction, feeling the joy of heaven intensified by the sight of the suffering souls in hell. It is a satisfaction to tell you that the suffering souls, and their hell, are but fictitious things created by the imagination from the astral substance—a mere stage setting as it were. Dante's Inferno has its adequate counterparts on the Astral Plane.

I ask you, particularly to gaze upon this most horrible scene before us. A large severely furnished edifice is shown, with seated congregation wearing stern, hard, cruel faces. They gaze toward the top of a smoking bottomless pit, from which rises a sort of great, endless chain, each link having a huge sharp hook upon which is impaled a doomed soul. This soul is supposed to rise to the top of the pit once in a thousand years, and as each appears it is heard to cry in mournful accents: "How long—how long?" To this agonized question, a deep stern voice is heard replying: "Forever! Forever!" I am glad to tell you that this congregation is dwindling, many evolving to higher conceptions, and practically no new recruits arriving from the earth-plane to fill the depleting ranks. In time, this congregation will disappear entirely, and the ghastly stage scenery and properties will gradually dissolve into astral dust and fade from sight forever.

All forms of religion, high and low, oriental and occidental, ancient and modern, are represented on this plane. Each has its own particular abode. It would delight the heart of a student of comparative religion to visit these scenes. There are some beautiful and inspiring scenes and regions on this plane, filled with advanced souls and beautiful characters. But, alas! there are some repulsive ones also. It is marvellous, in viewing these scenes, to realize how many forms human religion and theology has taken in its evolution. Every form of deity has its region, with its worshippers. It is interesting to visit the scenes once filled with the worshippers of the most ancient religions. Many have only a handful of worshippers remaining on this plane; while in some cases, the worshippers have entirely disappeared, and the astral scenery of the region, its temples and shrines, are crumbling away and disappearing just as have the old temples disappeared on the material plane.

On the highest of the sub-planes of the Astral we find many regions inhabited by the philosophers, scientists, metaphysicians, and higher theologians of the race—those who used their intellectual power in striving to solve the Riddle of the Universe, and to peer Behind the Veil, by the use of intellect alone. High and low are met with here. There are as many schools of philosophy and metaphysics here, as there were religious sects on the plane below.

Some are pitifully weak, crude and childish in their conceptions—others have advanced so far that they seem like demi-gods of intellect. But even this is not true "spirituality," any more than is the religious formalism and dogmas of the plane below. All has its place, however, and everything is evolving and unfolding.

It is interesting to note then on this plane, and the one below, are to be found groups of disembodied souls who persist in declaring that "there is no hereafter for the soul;" "the soul perishes with the body;" etc. These deluded souls believe that they are still on the material plane, in spite of appearances, and they have built up quite a good counterfeit earth-scenery to sustain them. They sneer and sniff at all talk of life outside of the physical body, and bang their astral tables with their astral fists, to prove how solid all real things are—they believe only that which is solid and "real." This, indeed, is the very irony of astral life.

You have noticed certain glorious forms on these regions, student, as we have passed through these scenes, and I have promised to inform you as to their character. These were those highly evolved beings, once men like ourselves, who have voluntarily returned from higher spheres to teach and instruct along the lines of religion and philosophy, combining the best of both, and leading upward toward Truth those souls who have arrived at a possible understanding of these things. It is verily true, on the Astral as well as on the earth plane, that "when the pupil is ready, the Master appears." The Astral has many, very many of these Elder Brothers of the Race, working diligently and earnestly for the uplift of those struggling on the Path.

I may say here, that an understanding of the nature of the various regions of the Astral, and the scenes thereof, will throw light upon the fact that the reports of "the other side" given by disembodied souls at spiritualistic seances, etc., are so full of contradictions and discrepancies, no two seeming to agree. The secret is that each is telling the truth as he sees it in the Astral, without realizing the nature of what they have seen, or the fact that it is, at the best, merely one aspect among millions of others. Contrast the varying ."heavens" just mentioned, and see how different the reports would be coming from some of their inhabitants. When the nature of astral phenomena is once understood, the difficulty vanishes, and each report is recognized as being an attempt to describe the Astral picture upon which the disembodied entity has gazed, believing it to be actual and real.

I wish here to tell you, student, some little about the planes higher than the Astral. These planes transcend adequate description. Enough to say, here, that each soul on the Astral, even the very lowest, finally sinks into an astral slumber when it has completed its work on that plane. Before passing on to rebirth, however, it awakens for a time upon one of the subdivisions of the next highest plane above the Astral. It may remain awake on this plane, in its appropriate subdivision, for merely a moment of time, or for many centuries even, depending upon its state of spiritual unfoldment. During this stay on these higher planes, the soul communes with the higher phase of itself—the divine fragment of Spirit—and is strengthened and invigorated thereby. In this period of communion, much dross of the nature is burnt out and dissolved into nothingness, and the higher part of the nature is nourished and encouraged.

These higher planes of Being constitute the real "heaven world" of the soul. The more highly advanced the soul, the longer does it abide between incarnations on these planes. Just as the mind is developed and enabled to express its longings and ambitions, on the Astral, so is the higher portions of the soul strengthened and developed on these higher planes. The joy, happiness and spiritual blessedness of these higher planes are beyond ordinary words. So wonderful are they, that even long after the soul has been born again on earth, there will arise within it memories of its experiences upon those higher planes, and it will sigh for a return to them, as a dove sighs for its far-off home towards which its weary wings urge its flight. Once heard, the harmony of the heaven-world is never forgotten—its memories remain to strengthen us in moments of trial and sorrow.

These, then, are the real "heaven worlds" of the occult teachings—something far different from even the highest Astral planes. The reports of the mystics are based on experiences on these planes, not upon those of the Astral. Your soul has truly informed you regarding the reality of the existence of these wonderful regions and scenes—it has not deceived you. Therefore, hold fast to the ideal and the vision—follow the gleam, follow the gleam!

CHAPTER X.

THE ASTRAL LIGHT.

IT must not be supposed for a moment that the Astral is simply a plane of Nature created for a place of temporary abode and development for souls which have passed out of the physical body—a mere stopping place between reincarnations. Important as are the planes of the Astral in the progress of the disembodied souls, they form but one phase of the activities of this great plane of Nature. Indeed, even eliminating the disembodied souls from the Astral, there would be enough strange and wonderful phenomena on that plane, as well as enough wonderful inhabitants and dwellers on some of its subplanes, to still render it the place and region of interest that it always has been to occultists. Before we finish our astral journey, and return to earth life, let us take a hasty glance at these wonderful phases of astral phenomena and life.

THE ASTRAL LIGHT. Changing our vibrations, we find ourselves entering a strange region, the nature of which at first you fail to discern. Pausing a moment until your astral vision becomes attuned to the peculiar vibra-

tions of this region, you find that you are becoming gradually aware of what may be called
an immense picture gallery, spreading out in
all directions, and apparently bearing a direct
relation to every point of space on the surface
of the earth.

At first you find it difficult to decipher the
meaning of this great array of pictures. The
trouble arises from the fact that they are ar-
ranged not one after the other in sequence on
a flat plane, but rather in sequence, one after
another in a peculiar order which may be
called the order of "X-ness in space," because
it is neither the dimension of length, breadth,
or depth—it is practically the order of the
fourth dimension of space, which cannot be described in terms of ordinary spatial dimension.

Again, you find, upon closely examining the
pictures that they are very minute—practically
microscopic in size—and require the use of the
peculiar magnifying power of astral vision to
bring them up to a size capable of being recognized by your faculty of visual recognition.

The astral vision, when developed, is capable
of magnifying any object, material or astral, to
an enormous degree—for instance, the trained
occultist is able to perceive the whirling atoms
and corpuscles of matter, by means of this

peculiarity of astral vision. Likewise, he is able to plainly perceive many fine vibrations of light which are invisible to the ordinary sight. In fact, the peculiar Astral Light which pervades this region is due to the power of the astral vision to receive and register these fine vibrations of light.

Bring this power of magnifying into operation, you will see that each of the little points and details of the great world picture so spread before you in the Astral Light, is really a complete scene of a certain place on earth, at a certain period in the history of the earth. It resembles one of the small views in a series of moving pictures—a single view on the roll of film. It is fixed and not in motion, and yet we can move forward along the fourth dimension, and thus obtain a moving picture of the history of any point on the surface of the earth, or even combine the various points into a larger moving picture, in the same way. Let us prove this by actual experiment.

Close your eyes for a moment, while we travel back in time (so to speak) along the series of these astral records—for, indeed, they travel back to the beginning of the history of the earth. Now open your eyes! Looking around you, you perceive the pictured representation of strange scenes filled with persons wearing a peculiar garb—but all is still, no life, no motion.

Now, let us move forward in time, at a much higher rate than that in which the astral views were registered. You now see flying before you the great movement of life on a certain point of space, in a far distant age. From birth to death you see the life of these strange people, all in the space of a few moments. Great battles are fought, and cities rise before your eyes, all in a great moving picture flying at a tremendous speed.

Now stop, and then let us move backward in time, still gazing at the moving pictures. You see a strange sight, like that of "reversing the film" in a moving picture. You see everything moving backward—cities crumbling into nothingness, men rising from their graves, and growing younger each second until they are finally born as babes—everything moving backward in time, instead of forward.

You can thus witness any great historical event, or follow the career of any great personage from birth to death—or backward. You will notice, moreover, that everything is semi-transparent, and that accordingly, you can see the picture of what is going on inside of buildings as well as outside of them. Nothing escapes the Astral Light Records. Nothing can be concealed from it.

You have gazed at the great World Picture in the Records of the Astral Light—the great Akashic Records, as we Hindus call it. In these records are to be found pictures of every single event, without exception, that has ever happened in the history of the earth—recorded just exactly as it really happened, moreover, the record being ultra-photographic and including the smallest detail.

By travelling to a point in time, on the fourth dimension, you may begin at that point, and see a moving picture of the history of any part of the earth from that time on to the present— or you may reverse the sequence by travelling backward, as we have seen. You may also travel in the Astral, on ordinary space dimensions, and thus see what happened simultaneously all over the earth, at any special moment of time, if you wish.

As a matter of strict truth, however, I must inform you that the real records of the past— the great Akashic Records—really exist on a much higher plane than the Astral, and that which you have witnessed is but a reflection (practically perfect, however) of the original records.

It requires a high degree of occult development in order to perceive even this reflection in the Astral Light, and unaided by my own power you could not perceive these sights at this time. An ordinary clairvoyant, however, is often able to catch occasional glimpses of these astral pictures, and may thus describe fairly well the happenings of the past. In the same way, the psychometrist, given an object, may be able to give the past history of the object, including a description of the persons associated therewith.

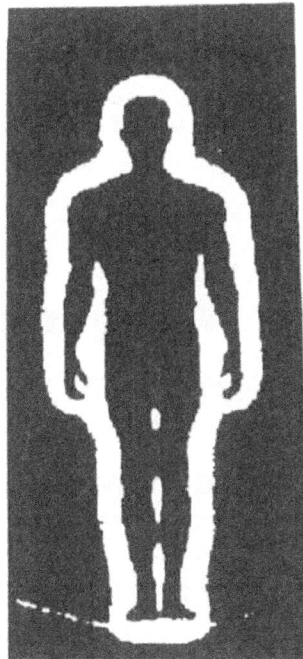

CHAPTER XI.

ASTRAL ENTITIES.

WITHOUT intending to go deeply into this subject—for the same is reserved for the sole teaching of the advanced pupil, and must not be carelessly spread before others—I think it well to call your attention to the fact that on certain planes of the Astral, there exist certain entities, or living beings, which never were human, and never will be, for they belong to an entirely different order of nature.

These strange entities are ordinarily invisible to human beings, but under certain conditions they may be sensed by the astral vision. Strictly speaking, these strange beings do not dwell upon the Astral at all—that is, not in the sense of the Astral as a part of space, or a place. We call them Astral entities simply because they become visible for the first time to man, when he is able to vision on the Astral, or by means of the astral senses—and for no other reason.

So far as place, or space, is concerned these entities or being dwell upon the earth, just as do the human beings. They vibrate differently from us, that is all. They are also usually of but a microscopic size, and would be invisible to the human eye even if they vibrated on the same plane as do we. The astral vision not only senses their vibrations, under certain conditions, but also, under certain other conditions, it magnifies their forms into perceptible size.

Some of these astral entities are known as Nature Spirits, and inhabit streams, rocks, mountains, forests, etc. Their occasional appearance to persons of psychic temperament, or in whom a degree of astral vision has been awakened, has given rise to the numerous tales and legends in the folk-lore of all nations regarding a strange order of beings, to which various names have been given, as for instance: fairies, pixies, elves, brownies, peris, djinns, trolls, satyrs, fauns, kobolds, imps, goblins, little folk, tiny people, etc., etc., and similar names found in the mythologies and legends of all people. The old occultists called the earth entities of this class by the name of "gnomes;" the air entities as "sylphs;" the water beings as "undines;" and the fire, or ether, beings as "salamanders."

This class of astral entities, as a rule, avoid the presence of man, and fly from places in which he dwells—for instance they avoid large cities as men avoid a cemetery. They prefer the solitudes of nature, and resent the onward march of men which drives them further and further into new regions. They do not object to the physical presence of man, so much as they do his mental vibrations which are plainly felt by them, and which are very distasteful to them.

A certain class of them are what may be called "good fellows," and these, once in a while, seem to find pleasure in helping and aiding human beings to whom they have formed an attachment. Many such cases are related in the folk lore of the older countries, but modern life has driven these friendly helpers from the scene, in most places.

Another class, now also very uncommon, seems to find delight in playing elfish, childish pranks, particularly in the nature of practical jokes upon peasants, etc. At spiritualistic seances, and similar places, these elfish pranks are sometimes in evidence.

The ancient magicians and wonder workers were often assisted by creatures of this class. And, even today in India, Persia, China, and other Oriental lands, such assistance is not unknown; and many of the wonderful feats of these magicians are attributable only to such aid.

As a rule, as I have said, these creatures are not unfriendly to man, though they may play a prank with him occasionally, under some circumstances. They seem particularly apt to play tricks upon neophytes in psychic research, who seek to penetrate the Astral without proper instruction, and without taking the proper precautions. To such a one they may appear as hideous forms, monsters, etc., and thus drive him away from the plane in which their presence may become apparent to him.

However, they usually pay no attention to the advanced occultist, and either severely let him alone, or else flee his presence—though cases are not unknown, in the experience of the majority of advanced occultists, when some of these little folk seem anxious and willing to be of aid to the earnest, conscientious inquirer, who recognizes them as a part of nature's great manifestation, and not as an "unnatural" creature, or vile monstrosity.

ARTIFICIAL ENTITIES.. In addition to the non-human entities which are perceived by astral vision, or on the Astral plane—including a number of varietites and classes other than those mentioned by me, and to which I pur-

posely have omitted reference for reasons
which will be recognized as valid by all true
occultists—there are to be found on the Astral,
or on the earth plane by means of astral vision,
a great class of entities, or semi-entities,
which occultists know as "artificial entities."

These artificial entities were not born in the
natural manner, nor created by the ordinary
creative forces of nature. They are the crea-
tions of the minds of men, and are really a
highly concentrated class of thought-forms.
They are not entities, in the strict sense of the
term, having no life or vitality except that
which they borrow from, or have been given by
their creators. The student of occultism who
has grasped the principle of the creation of
thought-forms, will readily grasp the nature,
power, and limitations of this class of dwellers
in the Astral.

The majority of these artificial entities, or
thought-forms, are created unconsciously by
persons who manifest strong desire-force, accompanied by definite mental pictures of that
which they desire. But many have learned the
art of creating them consciously, in an elementary form of magic, white or black. Much
of the effect of thought-force, or mind-power,
is due to the creation of these thought-forms.

Strong wishes for good, as well as strong curses for evil, tend to manifest form and a semblance of vitality in the shape of these artificial entities. These entities, however, are under the law of thought-attraction, and go only where they are attracted. Moreover, they may be neutralized, and even destroyed, by positive thought properly directed in the way known to all advanced students along these lines.

Another, and quite a large, class of these artificial Astral entities, consist of thought-forms of supernatural (!) beings, sent out by the strong mental pictures, oft repeated, of the persons creating them—the creator usually being unconscious of the result. For instance, a strongly religious mother, who prays for the protective influence of the angels around and about her children, and whose strong religious imagination pictures these heavenly visitors as present by the side of the children, frequently actually creates thought-forms of such angel guardians around her children, who are given a degree of life and mind vibrations from the soul of the mother. In this way, such guardian angels, so created, serve to protect the children and warn them from evil and against temptation. Many a pious mother has accomplished more than she realized by her prayers and earnest desires. The early fathers of the churches, occidental and oriental, were aware of this fact, and consequently bade their followers to use this form of prayer and thought, though they did not explain the true underlying reason. Even after the mother has passed on to higher planes, her loving memory may serve to keep alive these thought-form entities, and thus serve to guard her loved ones.

In a similar way, many "family ghosts" have been created and kept in being in the same way, by the constantly repeated tale and belief in their reality, on the part of generation after generation. In this class belong the celebrated historic ghosts who warn royal or noble families of approaching death or sorrow. The familiar family ghosts walking the walls of old castles on certain anniversaries, are usually found to belong to this class (though not always so).

Many haunted houses are explained in this way, also—the ghost may be "laid" by anyone familiar with the laws of thought-forms. It must be remembered that these artificial entities are of purely human creation, and obtain all their apparent and mind from the action of the thought-force of their creators. Repeated thought, and repeated belief, will serve to keep alive and to strengthen these entities—otherwise they will disappear in time.

Many supernatural visitors, saints, semi-divine beings, etc., of all religions have been formed in this way, and, in many cases, are kept in being by the faith of the devotees of the church, chapel, or shrine. In many temples in oriental countries, there have been created, and kept alive for many centuries, the thought-form entities of the minor gods and saints, endowed in thought with great power of response to prayer, offering, and ceremonies. Those accepting the belief in these powers, are brought into harmony with its vibrations, and are effected thereby, for good or evil.

The power of the devils of savage races (some of whom practically are devil-worshippers), arise in the same way. Even in the early history of the western religions, we find many references to the appearance of the Devil, and of his evil work; witchcraft diabolical presences, etc., all of which were created thought-form entities of this kind. Many of the effects of sorcery, black-magic, etc., were produced in this way—the element of belief, of course, adding greatly to the effect. The Voodoo practices of Africa, and later, of Martinique; and the Kahuna practices of Hawaii, are based on these same principles. The effect of "charms," etc., depend on the same laws, including the effect of faith.

Even certain forms of "spirits," so-called, of certain forms of spiritualistic seances arise from this principle, and have never been human beings, at all. An understanding of this principle will aid in the interpretation of many puzzling phases of psychic phenomena.

"SPIRIT RETURN." Nothing that I have said must be taken as denying the reality and validity of what the western world knows as "spirit return." On the other hand, I am fully familiar with very many instances of the real return to earth-life of disembodied souls. But at the same time, I, as well as all other advanced occultists, are equally aware of the many chances of mistake in this class of psychic phenomena. Shades, and even astral shells, too often are mistaken for departed loved ones. Again, many apparently real "spirit forms" are nothing more or less than semi-vitalized thought-form artificial entities such as I have just described.

Again, many mediums are really clairvoyant, and are able to unconsciously draw to some extent upon the Astral Records for their information regarding the past, instead of receiving the communication from a disembodied soul—in all honesty and in good faith, in many cases. Occultism does not deny the phenomena of modern western spiritualism—it merely seeks to explain its true nature, and to verify some of it while pointing out the real nature of others. It should be welcomed as an ally, by all true spiritualists.

ASTRAL VISION. It must not be supposed that the astral vision dawns suddenly upon anyone, in full force. Rather is it a matter of slow gradual development in the majority of cases. Many persons possess it to a faint degree, and fail to develop it further, for want of proper instruction. Many persons have occasional flashes of it, and are entirely without it at other times. Many "feel" the astral vibrations, rather than seeing with the astral vision. Others, gain a degree of astral vision by means of crystal gazing, etc. That which is frequently referred to as "psychic sight," or "psychic sensing," is a form of astral visioning or sensing. Psychism is bound up with astral phenomena, in all cases.

* * * * * * * *

In this little manual, I have sought to give

you, in a few lines, the great underlying facts of the Astral Plane. I have crowded very much into a very small space, so that you will have to read and study my words very carefully, in order to get the full meaning. In fact, this is not a book to be read on and then laid aside—rather, it should be re-read and re-studied, until all the essence is extracted.

* * * * * * * *

The glimpses of a number of the sub-planes of the Astral should give you a general, clear idea of many other scenes on that great plane. Remember, these scenes are typical of those witnessed by any advanced occultist who is able to travel on those planes—as you, yourself, may verify when you are able to vision on these planes. They are under-drawn, rather than overdrawn. Some of the more startling and "sensational" scenes have been omitted altogether, as I have no desire to attract, or cater to, those seeking sensation—my work is for the earnest student, alone.

* * * * * * * *

Use this manual as a key to unlock many mysteries—not as a book to while away an idle hour. Do not have any "idle hours." Do not try to "kill time." Be an earnest, thoughtful, occultist, ever unfolding and evolving as you progress along The Path! Look Forward, not Backward! Look Upward, not Downward! Have Faith, not Fear! For, within your soul is a Spark of the Divine Flame, which cannot be extinguished!

The Ultimate Mystery: Are UFOs Dimensional Machines?

By Tim R. Swartz

USING your mind to influence time-space to the extent that the dimensional field could be broached has been the subject of occult theory for many centuries. However, in this modern age, mind power has been circumnavigated by science. Is it possible that other dimensions could be accessed using technology? Have some highly unusual cases of UFO/human interaction demonstrated that UFOs may be operating outside the realm of normal time and space?

For most people, spotting a UFO would be considered extremely unusual, but for two Ohio women, seeing a UFO was the least surprising part of their experience.

In June 2001, two sisters, Angie Whitmeyer and Deborah Simmons, were returning from a day of shopping in Dayton, Ohio, when a strange light in the sky caught their attention.

"We were heading home to Kingman, Ohio, on State Road 73," Deborah recalled. "It was a beautiful evening around 8:30 p.m., the air was warm and the sky crystal clear. Angie was driving and I was watching the scenery go by when I noticed a bright light in the western sky."

Deborah watched in amazement as the light grew in intensity and flew towards the car at an incredible speed.

"Deborah asked me what that weird light was," said Angie. "But we were close to Caesar Creek Lake and the road was pretty dark so I wasn't paying a lot of attention to it. But then it flew right in front of us so I couldn't miss it."

How To Travel To Other Dimensions

The bright light soared past the car and hovered over the nearby treetops, casting an eerie glow over the entire area. Whitmeyer pulled the car over onto the side of the road so they could get a better look at the unusual object.

Deborah was shocked by how large and close the UFO was to them: "The light was so bright and white that you couldn't see any shape behind it. But we could tell it was pretty big, at least as big as a house. The funny thing was that I couldn't hear any sort of engine like you would normally hear with an airplane or helicopter. It was completely silent."

Suddenly, another, identical bright light swooped down from the sky and hovered a short distance away. The two sisters decided the situation was becoming too strange and tried to drive away.

"That's when I discovered that the car had stopped and I couldn't restart it," Angie said. "Nothing worked, the lights, the radio, it was completely dead."

The two women also noticed an odd silence had descended over the area, accompanied by a strange feeling of isolation. Angie remembered that it seemed as if they were the only people in the world.

"I don't remember seeing another car come by during the entire time we were there, which is really weird because at that time of an evening there's always traffic on that road. And it was just dead silent outside, no birds, nothing. It was as if we were in another world."

Uncertain what to do next, Angie and her sister continued to watch the strange pair of lights when, unexpectedly, both objects shot straight up and disappeared into the night sky. The area was plunged into darkness, and oddly enough, the normal sounds of the night came back almost as if switched on.

"As soon as the lights flew away," Deborah said, "the car started running again all by itself. The lights and radio were on just as they were before everything happened."

How To Travel To Other Dimensions

According to their watches, the strange encounter had lasted more than 20 minutes. However, when they arrived home, Deborah's husband seemed unconcerned about what they thought was a late arrival. That's when they discovered that instead of being after 9:00 p.m., as their wristwatches indicated, it was only 8:35 p.m.

"It was as if the entire time we spent looking at those lights had never happened," Angie said. "But it did happen, our watches both showed we had been stuck out there for over 20 minutes, but somehow we gained that time back with a few minutes to spare. Normally we should have been home at around ten to nine, but somehow, despite what had happened, we got there early."

Distortions in Time and Space

One of the strangest aspects of some UFO encounters is the apparent distortion of time when a UFO is nearby. Researchers and writers have tried for years to understand and to interpret what happens before, during, and after a close contact with a UFO. But, many reports of time anomalies have been kept off some UFO databases because such events fall outside of the preconceived notions of what a UFO sighting should entail.

Like the two Ohio sisters, others who have experienced a close contact with a UFO have reported apparent time distortions like the failure of car engines, a strange feeling of isolation (to the point where it is observed that no other vehicles or people are seen during the sighting), unusual silence, spatial changes, altered states of consciousness, and distortions in the flow of time.

Donald Pilz, of the Tri-Core Research group suggests that UFOs use a characteristic black aperture, the "softspot" to enter/exit our atmosphere.

"The transient time distortion effects commonly reported with close proximity UFO sightings must be associated with the unknown energy field that is emitted from the craft and or the waves that are emitted from the soft spot opening. I have suggested that the soft spot is in fact a huge gravity wave distortion that bends light back towards itself, hence appearing black. In conventional physics it is considered possible for immense gravity fields to slow time. I suspect that there is an immensely powerful "inert motionless time-field" created around both the soft spot and the UFO craft that does indeed alter our atmospheric mass (molecules, atoms, electrons, protons, etc) so that it all becomes an inert time-field. If for an aerial object; the sheer size of this "inert energy field" extended itself all the way down to the earth's surface, it might just explain the time distortion and paralysis effects felt by some of the observers. If the field strength is of highly variable intensity and distribution when it touches the ground then this might explain why the majority of UFO cases do not feature this phenomenon. Could these special fields of null time resemble the packed isobars of atmospheric pressure for a ground witness to experience the exact conditions inside the soft spot? This action of this extended grounded time-field might also explain another more commonly reported type of effect from UFO sightings; the total absence of sounds or natural noises while observing the event. Some observers recall that there was an umbrella of total silence when the craft or opening was present, and that these everyday sounds immediately returned to normal when the craft and or opening disappeared."

Generally, these anomalies disappear along with the UFO. Occasionally, however, the witnesses will suffer from unexpected relapses weeks, even years, after the initial experience.

These anomalous events have created more headaches than answers for researchers who have attempted to find scientific validation for unusual UFO encounters. On the surface, some of the reported anomalies seem to be explainable using modern science. However, upon closer analysis, strange things tend to become even stranger.

Failure of Car Engines

The disruption of car motors, machinery, and electronic devices during a UFO event has been commonly reported. Thousands of these inexplicable stories have been duly recorded over the years and many volumes have been written in an attempt to understand the underlying principles involved.

Mark Rodeghier of the Center for UFO Studies analyzed 441 cases in which "the car, truck, or other motor vehicle in which a witness was either riding or in near proximity to, was seemingly affected by the presence of a UFO. Headlights, radios and even flashlights were also affected."

Of the vehicle failure cases summarized by Rodeghier, ten percent noted an unusual phenomenon called "spontaneous engine restarts" at the end of a sighting. In reality, this figure is probably much higher considering the amount of underreported and under-documented cases worldwide.

In these cases the car's engine would mysteriously restart without the driver turning the key. One witness said: "As soon as the UFO flew away, the car, radio, headlights, switched back on by themselves. One second everything was completely dead, and the next, everything was running smoothly as if nothing had ever happened."

The witness said he was left with the feeling that his car had been stopped between the ticks of a clock: "Like time had completely vanished."

The Oz Effect

Another notable feature of many cases is the sudden unusual silence and an overwhelming feeling of isolation in the proximity of a UFO. Many people have noted that normal sounds—birds, insects, and traffic — suddenly stop just before and during a close UFO sighting.

A man from Wisconsin reported that he had observed a UFO hovering over the treetops directly over his head once while deer hunting. He stated that the day had been windy and the trees were swaying and creaking pretty loudly in the breeze. What made him look up was the fact that all of a sudden the forest went "completely dead."

He noted that the trees had stopped moving as if "frozen in place." That is when he noticed a strange, dark, triangle-shaped object floating over the trees.

"It was a little bigger than a pickup truck and was solid black. I didn't see any lights or hear any kind of sound from it."

The hunter reported feeling like he was "looking up through a tunnel with me at the bottom and the UFO at the top. I knew that I was completely alone and that no one could help me."

How To Travel To Other Dimensions

As soon as the UFO passed overhead the forest returned to normal.

The experience of such unusual sensations around a UFO has been dubbed "the Oz Effect" by UFO researcher and author Jenny Randles, and may indicate that there could be a field of influence that is being emitted around a UFO. Anyone close enough to a UFO would find himself completely contained within this field. The odd effects noticed by eyewitnesses could give us some kind of indication of the true nature of these energy fields. Unfortunately, anecdotal accounts of UFO experiences have rarely been followed up with rigorous studies of their content.

UFOs and Time

Scientists brave (or foolhardy) enough to try and conduct proper research on the nature of UFOs have been unable to find satisfactory answers as to why UFOs seem to cause time distortions. Past interpretations of Einstein's physics leave little room for localized time anomalies, unless influenced by a gravitationally massive object such as a black hole.

However, the new kids on the physics block, quantum and string theories may show that time and space is easier to influence than was previously thought. Some physicists believe that it is possible to engineer space-time itself and to surround a spaceship with a local space-time in such a way that locally, the light barrier remains intact, while from the outside the ship is moving at faster-than-light velocity. UFOs that seem to rapidly accelerate, change direction, or even disappear are actually operating conservatively from the viewpoint of their own internal time rates.

If someone or something came close enough to a ship that was creating its own space-time, normal time and space, as they know it, would cease to exist for them, and they would come under the influence of the artificial space-time.

This could explain some of the stranger aspects of UFO encounters, such as environmental sounds disappearing, isolation, the freezing of motors and electronic devices, and the feeling of time slowing down, stretching out, and losing all meaning. The UFO is literally creating an alteration in the local state of space-time, thus generating a major distortion effect that is experienced by the witness. Within this time anomaly the perceived forward motion of time could even disappear, allowing for the past, present, and future to intrude upon one another.

A Glimpse of the Past

In 1981, Linda Taylor and her mother were traveling by car to Chorlton, a district of Manchester, England. The normally busy road became strangely empty and the two women noticed a huge light in the sky that seemed to pace their car.

Linda told investigators that her car "jerked about" and slowed down despite her attempts to accelerate. Suddenly, an "old-fashioned" car appeared in the road ahead and drove straight towards the two women. At the same time the light in the sky turned into a metal disc that hovered over the main road.

As the UFO moved away from Taylor and her mother, the old car vanished instantly. When the women returned home they found that two hours were missing from their trip. As with some others who have had close UFO encounters, Linda later had several odd psychic experiences and further time lapses.

Time distortions may not always occur with a visible UFO nearby. In 1980, Peter Rojcewicz, now a professor of humanities and folklore at New York's Juilliard School, was in the University of Pennsylvania library reading a UFO book suggested by another professor.

As he read, Rojcewicz noticed that someone was standing in front of him. Looking up, Rojcewicz saw a very gaunt, pale man, about six feet tall and weighing around 140 pounds. The strange man wore a black suit, black shoes, a black string tie, and a bright white shirt. His suit was loose and it looked as though he had slept in it for days.

"He sat down like he had dropped from the ceiling—all in one movement— and folded his hands on top of a stack of books in front of him," Rojcewicz said.

How To Travel To Other Dimensions

The man asked Rojcewicz what he was doing. Rojcewicz said he was reading about flying saucers.

"Have you seen a flying saucer?" the man asked. Rojcewicz said he hadn't.

"Do you believe in the reality of flying saucers?" Rojcewicz said he didn't know much about them and wasn't sure he was very interested in the phenomena.

The man screamed: "Flying saucers are the most important fact of the century and you are not interested?"

The man then stood up, again, all in a single awkward movement, put his hand on Rojcewicz's shoulder, and said: "Go well on your purpose." With that, he left.

Rojcewicz was suddenly overwhelmed by fear: "I had a sense that this man was out of the ordinary and that idea frightened me. I got up and walked around the stacks toward where the reference librarians usually are. The librarians weren't there. There were no guards there—there was nobody else in the library...I was utterly alone and terrified."

The professor went back to the table where he had been reading "to get myself together. It took me about an hour. Then I got up and everything was back to normal; the people were all there."

It would seem that Rojcewicz could have been placed into a separate time-space field in order for his contact to occur. The entire episode may have occurred in the blink of an eye in normal time-space. But for Rojcewicz, an entire hour passed.

One gentleman, who reported his alleged UFO abduction on an Internet forum, said that when he was being returned from an abduction to the motel room where he was staying, he "noticed that there was a person in the parking lot below us (myself and several 'Grays,' were 'floating' in mid-air so I had a bird's eye view of the surroundings,) [who] seemed to be frozen in mid-step. Everything was dead quiet and nothing was moving. It was as if time had stopped or frozen for the few moments it took for them to transport me from a UFO back to my room that was located on the second floor of the motel."

How To Travel To Other Dimensions

Another fascinating story comes from the son of the late Col Philip Corso, author of the groundbreaking book "The Day After Roswell." Not many people know that Philip Corso Jr. has gone on the record stating that he knows a great deal more about the Roswell incident than what was published in his father's book. In 2004 Phil Corso Jr. spoke with the co-author of "*The Day After Roswell*," William Birnes, at Stephen Bassett's X-Conference. The emphasis of the information was that the Roswell craft was not an extraterrestrial spacecraft, but instead was a time machine.

Phil Corso Jr. revealed that the so-called Extraterrestrial Biological Entities - contained two brains. One was organic and was believed to control the beings, and one was "laced with crystal electronics" and was thought to connect the beings with the craft - through time. It is purported that these beings are essentially Artificial Intelligences from our own future - and that their "crash" caused a bifurcation of our time-lines and altered our history. The most mind-boggling aspect of this story is that as a result of this time-line split and the subsequent advancement in technology from reverse-engineering that we are now on a time-line of technological evolution that will eventually create the very same craft and beings that actually crashed in Roswell in 1947.

These interesting cases show that there is still a lot we have to learn from UFO reports. Investigators need to be willing to look beyond the traditional "by-the-book" questions and allow the witnesses to relate their entire experience—no matter how unusual it may be. Many researchers and databases fail to mention some of the stranger aspects of UFO encounters because they don't fit a particular belief system or bias. We can learn much more if researchers put aside their own personal feelings and allow the full information to come forward.

Currently, any theories and conclusions are really little more than speculation. Nevertheless, scientists who are not afraid to look beyond the norm are every day developing new concepts in physics and the true nature of reality.

Parting the Dimensional Curtain with Black Boxes
By Commander X

THEY are known as Radionics, Ocilloclasts, Hieronymus machines, or more simply, black boxes. They allegedly use ancient techniques wrapped with the trappings of electricity and machinery of the modern era. This highly controversial field claims to detect and modulate life force using electronics, and numerous devices using these principals have been built and operated over the years.

Black boxes using radionics can be traced back to the early 20th century, but the technique call radiesthesia quite possibly has roots as far back as ancient Egypt. Radiesthesia is a branch of the ancient method of finding water called dowsing (water-witching) through hand-held devices such as a forked stick, L-rods and pendulums.

The oldest known document about dowsing is a Chinese engraving from the year 147 BC. The engraving shows the Emperor Yu (Hia dynasty, 2200 BC) holding in his hand an instrument shaped like a tuning fork. An inscription on the engraving states: "Yu, of the Hia dynasty, was famous for his knowledge of the presence of mineral deposits and sources; he could find concealed objects; he was able by his expertise to adapt the operation of the field according to the different seasons."

Dowsing can be used to find more than just water, it has also been successfully used to uncover precious metals, minerals, oil, missing persons and in making medical diagnosis and proscribing treatments. Nowadays practitioners are divided into two camps, that of physical radiesthesia and mental radiesthesia.

How To Travel To Other Dimensions

Followers of the physical theory define radiesthesia as a phenomenon that can be explained the laws of physics. They believe that everything encountered in nature, without exception, is a vibration, and that radiesthesia, like a radio receiver, can be used to detect this vibration. However, it is the instrument used by the diviner (the rod, pendulum, or black box) and not the diviner himself who succeeds in capturing the vibration.

By contrast, mental radiesthesia is supposed to receive its information using psychic abilities and intuition. The practitioner of radiesthesia makes contact with the target object or person using his subconscious. Next, his mind follows a conscious and an unconscious procedure which makes it possible for him to find the target object, diagnose a medical condition, and with a black box, attempt a cure or other desire result. In difference with the physical theory, the mental theory places the operator and not the device in the central position.

Abbe Alexis Bouly

One of the first medical dowsers was L'Abbe Alexis Bouly, a Catholic priest who lived at the turn of the 20th century in a little French seaside village on the English Channel. For years Bouly successfully dowsed for water and assisted in finding wells for French manufacturers. News of his success spread across the continent and he was contracted to find water for large factories in Belgium, Poland and Romania.

Bouly eventually founded the Society of Friends of Radiesthesie, a euphemism for "dowsing" using amalgam of a Latin root for 'radiation' and a Greek root for 'perception.' It literally means "perception of radiation." Seeking to find new uses for radiesthesia, Bouly began to study the world of microbial vibrations.

"I was bold enough to tackle it," he once wrote, "but to start with I had to learn about microbes, to study their nature and their influence on the human body."

In the hospitals of Boulogne-Sur-Mer, Berck-Plage, Lille, and in the Belgium City of Liege, Bouly carried out experiments to see if he could

Abbe Alexis Bouly

detect and identify microbes by using a pendulum. In repeated tests, Bouly was able to correctly identify different cultures of microbes in test tubes.

In 1950, in recognition of his accomplishments, at the age of 85, Bouly was made a Chevalier de La Legion d'Honneur, the highest decoration his nation could bestow on him.

A second medical dowsing pioneer was Father Jean-Louis Bourdoux, who spent sixteen years as a missionary in the jungles of Brazil's Matto Grosso. Due to the success of local plants to cure two almost fatal illnesses, Bourdoux decided to study the medical properties of Brazilian plants in order to help his fellow missionaries care for the sick. However, he was stumped with the question on how missionaries could be taught which plants in a particular area could act as specific remedies for specific ailments.

As fate would have it, during his research Bourdoux met Father Alexis Mermet who had learned to dowse for water from his grandfather and father. Mermet had concluded that if what lay hidden in the earth and in inanimate objects could be studied with a pendulum, then why couldn't the same pendulum detect hidden conditions in animals and human beings?

With Father Mermets help, Bourdoux eventually published his ***Practical Notions of Radiesthesia for Missionaries***. In the preface he wrote: "If you have the patience to read these pages you shall see how, thanks to the new science called 'radiesthesia,' you will be able, without any medical training and hardly any funds, to succor both believers and pagans. Perhaps you will be amazed at some of the things I have set down and be tempted to say: 'That's impossible.' But are we not living in a time of marvelous discoveries each more disconcerting than the next?"

Another priest who was interested in diagnosing and curing illnesses using radiesthesia was Father Jean Jurion who was introduced to dowsing in 1930 by a fellow priest. After WWII, Father Jurion, who was inspired by Bouly and Bourdoux, began to seriously study the use of dowsing in medicine.

Jurion started researching available literature about dowsing, but unfortunately he found a jumble of contradictory opinions that served only to muddy the waters about dowsing methods. Dowsing guides were filled with bad information such as not dowsing unless you were facing north or while wearing rubber-soled shoes. Another stated that one should always remove metallic objects before dowsing.

Jurion decided to ignore what he called a conglomeration of 'self-imposed servitude,' and found that he could dowse anywhere, any time, and under any conditions. When he began his own first attempts at diagnosis, he obtained excellent results that were confirmed by doctors. His greatest surprise was when he realized that his most dramatic achievements were related to cases that he thought were almost impossible to solve because doctors had given up on them.

One particularly difficult case was a 49-year-old Belgian man whose X-rays had confirmed that he had two inoperable tumors in his brain. The man had been given cobalt radiation treatments accompanied by x-rays, but the cancer continued to spread.

With the help of a pendulum, Jurion diagnosed homeopathic remedies for the man, and after one year doctors found that he was freed of the cancer. Jurion wrote, "...this diagnosis and treatment, which medical specialists could not believe would be effective, amply justifies the existence of the radiesthesia practitioner, who may not be a doctor, but may be a patient's last chance. It is our duty to take even the seemingly most intractable cases."

Unfortunately, Jurion was harassed for years and was taken to court numerous times as a result of complaints by the Order of Physicians. He would write at the time: "Since they treated me like an outlaw, I have written the book, *Journal of an Outlaw*, because I care for the sick without a medical degree, and they classify me with embezzlers, con men, and murderers." This would not be the last time the medical profession would attempt to repress the research and use of radiesthesia.

Radionics

It is only natural that practitioners of radiesthesia would look to science and technology to try and improve their methods. Since the 19th century mechanical devices using electricity had been built in an attempt to diagnosis and cure various illnesses. Even the great inventor Nikola Tesla had developed a line of medical devices using infra-red and electromagnetic frequencies that were widely used by doctors and hospitals.

Even though there were probably other machines built and used fitting the now accepted description of a black box, the first historically acknowledged black box was developed by Dr. Albert Abrams, an American neurologist from San Francisco. Dr. Abrams was a highly educated man with impeccable academic credentials from the University of Heidelberg where he garnered top honors and even a gold medal. In 1916 Abrams published *New Concepts in Diagnosis and Treatment*, and came up with the term radio therapy.

According to Dr. Abrams, all diseases have their own "vibratory rate" that can be measured and treated. Diseased body tissue affects the nervous system and produces 'dull emanations.' Dr. Abrams thought that an electrical phenomenon was involved and he invented a variable resistance instrument to measure the ohm resistance of different diseases on an electronic circuit.

With radio therapy it's thought that every person's energy patterns or rhythms are as unique to them as their fingerprints, and that every part of their body, down to the cell level, reflects these vibrations. When illness, injury, infection, stress, pollution, malnutrition, or poor hygiene cause these patterns to become imbalanced or interrupted the energy is altered. This altered energy pattern can be read from any part of the body and treated by sending messages, with an instrument, to the body in order that the body may heal itself through the restored flow of energy.

Abrams' diagnostic equipment consisted primarily of a variety of simple resistance boxes, often called Reflexophones, wired in series. A typical setup included the "dynamizer," which was a sample holder with 3 electrodes. The patient's blood sample on paper was placed on two electrodes to ground and the third electrode was connected to the "rheostatic dynamizer." This, in turn, was connected to the "vibratory rate rheostat," which was connected to the "measuring rheostat." The final connection was to an electrode on the forehead of a healthy third party. The healthy individual (called a reagent) would "react" biologically through the central nervous system to the diseased vibrations.

How To Travel To Other Dimensions

Dr. Albert Abrams

How To Travel To Other Dimensions

For example, Dr. Abrams found that cancer produced a 50 ohm resistance, while syphilis had a 55 ohm resistance. Abrams later modified his technique so he could take readings from a drop of blood.

Dr. Abrams had another device called an oscilloclast which he used to cure patients. This machine supposedly transmitted back at the diseased tissue the same electronic vibrations it was emitting until the patient was "clear" of the electronic reactions in the reagent.

The term "Radionics" was invented by students of Abrams by combining the two words "radiation" and "electronics." This implies that in radionics it is possible to measure a fine "radiation" with "electronic instruments" designed specifically for the purpose.

In 1924, the year of Abrams' death a committee of the Royal Society of Medicine under the Chairmanship of Sir Thomas (later Lord) Horder investigated his claims. To the astonishment of medicine and science, the committee, after exhaustive tests, had to admit that Abrams' devices did operate as claimed.

Nevertheless, Dr. Abrams and his black boxes was the subject of numerous investigations by the scientific and medical professions. Professor R A Millikan, Nobel Prize winner in physics and head of the California Institute of Technology, examined Abrams' apparatus and issued a statement to the effect that not only did the apparatus not rest on any sort of scientific foundation, but from the standpoint of physics were the height of absurdity.

Other physicists and engineers opened and investigated the devices and found them to be essentially a jungle of electric wires, violating all the sound rules of electronic construction. However, by 1925 there were more than 3,500 black box practitioners in the United States alone.

After Dr. Abrams death in 1924, the black box torch was picked up by Dr. Ruth Drown, a chiropractor based in Hollywood, California. Dr. Drown further developed Abrams' devices by replacing the human subject in the circuit with a sample of the person's blood or hair. It was called Radio-Vision. With the Down Radio-Vision Instrument there were two circuits involved, an 'assessment circuit' and a 'treatment circuit.' By removing the human subject from these circuits, Dr. Drown was able to both diagnose and treat patients at a distance. She referred to this technique as broadcasting, though it is more commonly known today as radionic projections.

According to Dr. Drown, the theory on which Radio-Vision is based is extremely simple. Fundamentally, the theory is based on the fact that everything having form in the physical world is made up of molecules. The molecular arrangement establishes the outer form of the substance. Because the molecular arrangements producing liver tissue for example, are different to the molecular arrangements producing lung tissue, liver tissue and lung tissue differ from each other in their outer form.

The molecules consist of whirling particles of electricity. This motion produces a definite emanation from all physical substances, which may be brought under direct observation through the specialized use of pinacyanole bromide filters and screens.

Differing molecular arrangements producing differing forms must also produce differing characteristic emanations in each case. In general terms, they produce differing frequencies or vibrations. These emanations may be detected and numerically classified on the Drown Diagnostic Instrument, also invented by Dr. Ruth Drown.

The Drown Diagnostic Instrument is a very simple impedance rheostat, consisting of nine dials, each of which can select ten tuning stubs by its rotation. Each dial is numbered from 1 to 10, each dial position making contact with a stub. The possible combinations permitted by this arrangement exceed two billion.

According to Dr. Drown and her followers, the Radio-Vision Instrument was not a machine that could be operated anyone. It was an instrument of high sensitivity intended for use by a thoroughly trained, competent and wise physician. However, in a University of Chicago demonstration, photos produced by a Radio-Vision device were explained away as fogging by momentarily exposing photographic plates to light.

Skeptics accused Dr. Drown of defrauding her patients and in 1951 she was tried on federal charges of introducing a misbranded device into interstate commerce. At the trial one of the government's expert witnesses, Dr. Elmer Belt, described the Drown device as "perfectly useless."

How To Travel To Other Dimensions

Dr. Drown was found guilty by the jury and was fined $1000. She stopped shipping her devices across state lines, but despite the setbacks and mistrust in the U.S., radionics has continued to develop and it is now accepted in several countries in Europe as an alternative medical treatment.

The Hieronymus Machine

Black boxes have continued to develop beyond the devices used only for medical diagnosis and treatment. Instruments for use in agriculture, mining, photography, and even more esoteric uses such as time travel, are being successfully used on a world-wide basis.

On September 27th, 1949 a U.S. patent was granted to Dr. Thomas Galen Hieronymous of Advanced Sciences Research and Development at Lakemont, Georgia. Dr. Hieronymus has the unique distinction of having the only U.S. patent of a psychically operating machine.

What Dr. Hieronymus invented was a machine to detect the type and quantity of any material under scrutiny by analyzing the radiation that emanates from all material; a radiation that he termed as "Eloptic" radiation. The word is taken from the first two letters of electricity and the word optic, because the energy has some, but not all, of the characteristics of both those forms of energy. His main idea was that the experimenter became a part of his own machine, bridging the physical and quantum worlds.

Eloptic energy radiates from or is in some manner given off from, or forms a force field around, everything in our material world under normal conditions at ordinary room temperature and without any treatment of any kind. Each element and combination of elements that make up our material world gives off this energy; however, the energy from each element differs in frequency from the radiation coming from every other element. Because of this, we have a means of determining the contents of an unknown material by analyzing the radiations from it without in any way destroying or disturbing the object or material in question, or having to excite it in any manner.

How To Travel To Other Dimensions

Patent number 2,482,773 was awarded after three years of careful study by the United States Patent Office. There are strict guidelines that must be observed before a patent is awarded. A "utility patent" for a machine must be something new, unusual, and unobvious. As well, the invention had to be useful for at least one authentic thing that could not be done before. Dr. Hieronymus did not need to explain how it worked, only to prove that it worked sufficiently enough to have undeniable merit.

With a patent application such as was submitted by Dr. Hieronymus, where an invention seems to defy the basic principles of science, extra proof is required. Hieronymus backed up his claims with live plant experiments and made working models of his invention.

The Hieronymous machine used a rubbing plate so that when it was tuned to resonance with the object being analyzed and when the circuitry sensed a "signal," the smooth connection between the operator's fingers and a touch pad became tacky or suddenly developed a sticky feel. Until this point the standard instrument indicator mechanism had been an audible sound or a visual indicator such as a needle deflection (as in a multimeter) or a flashing light.

The effect was rapid enough to prove useful as an alternative measuring mechanism. The device uses a very basic pickup coil, a simple three transistor amplifier (instead of valves) and a tuning device consisting of a rotating optical prism. The sample of metal or mineral to be analyzed is placed within the "sensing coil" and the mechanism is tuned with the rotating prism. The signal is then amplified and the output is fed to a flat coil of wire underneath a flat square of glass or plastic. This is the touch pad.

The fingertips are placed lightly on this pad and slowly moved back and forth while the tuning prism is being rotated. When the circuit is resonant, the feeling between the fingertips and the touchpad changes from smooth to sticky.

The dial of the machine is pre-calibrated for various known elements so when the sample of an unknown substance is placed in the pickup coil the presence of specific elements can be determined. Also the actual percentage of materials can be determined. Even more amazing is that

How To Travel To Other Dimensions

Eloptic energy can be conducted along light rays, focused with lenses, refracted with a prism and its effect implanted upon photographic film.

An aerial photograph film taken at several hundred thousand feet elevation can be used to determine what was in the objects photographed on the ground, such as people and metals in buildings, cars, etc.

The apparatus can be set for any elements such as iron, a stylus placed on the spot on the film to be analyzed, the energy implanted on the film can be picked up by the stylus, conducted through the instrument, and if there is the Eloptic energy of iron on the film it is evident that there was iron on the ground, radiating the characteristic iron frequency even though not visible to the eye.

Plants can be analyzed to determine whether the root, stem, or fruit contains the elements necessary for proper nutrition, such as iron, copper, manganese and other trace elements. The plant or fruit can also be analyzed to determine whether it contains arsenic or other poisons from sprays. Foods, poisons, drugs, etc., can be checked to determine their effect upon the body or any particular tissue of the body. Those foods or drugs to which a person is allergic and those which are compatible can then be quickly identified.

Just as a photograph can hold the emanation of the object photographed, so can a specimen, an article of clothing, a drop of blood, urine or perspiration carry the emanations of the person from where it came.

Such a specimen will carry all the emanations from all parts of the body of the person from whom the blood was taken. Its emanation and those taken directly from the body of the person will be the same. This way, many of the characteristics of the person from whom the blood or clothing came can be determined.

According to Dr. Hieronymous, Eloptic energy has desirable applications in the fields of: (1) Laboratory chemical analysis, (2) Mining, (3) Prospecting, (4) Medicine, (5) Nutrition, (6) Animal husbandry, (7) Horticulture, (8) Military intelligence, (9) Criminology, and (10) General betterment of humanity.

How To Travel To Other Dimensions

The former editor of *Analog Magazine*, John Campbell, once built a Hieronymus device and successfully tested it. Campbell recognized that modern physics couldn't explain how the device was able to operate. In an exchange with Arthur Young, Young suggested to Campbell that it was the mind of the operator that made the device function, and that it was the symbolic form of the device that dynamically functioned to make it work. This appeared particularly significant to Campbell since he had discovered he could make the device work even though disconnected from its power supply.

Campbell decided to test this thesis and he carefully drew on paper in a schematic diagram of the amplifier, removed the actual amplifier hardware, and substituted the schematic drawing. To his amazement, the device worked just as it had done before the amplifier was removed.

Unfortunately, these are the type of results that have earned Black Boxes the wraith of government agencies such as the FDA who have branded them all as fake and incapable of working as claimed. However, those who work with the devices present some compelling evidence to the otherwise.

In the Cumberland Valley, a scientist from the Pennsylvania Farm Bureau put a photo of an insect infested field into a Black Box; along with it they put a tiny amount of insecticide. Forty-eight hours later, the insects in the infected field, many miles away, were all dead. Because of this, the Farm Bureau wanted exclusive use of the device in Pennsylvania.

The Monterey County Farm Bureau said that they had been using radionic control on cotton...and found no occasion to use insecticide On untreated fields, however, their cost for insecticide was in excess of $26 an acre.

John Campbell wrote in **Analog** that: "This machine is almost pure magic! In the old real sense it cast spells, imposes death magic and can be used for life magic! The machine works beautifully."

Dr. Heironymus himself reportedly used his Black Box to monitor the life support systems of the Apollo astronauts. He successfully received all the correct data, before NASA did.

How To Travel To Other Dimensions

For anyone interested in working with a Black Box a positive attitude is all that is necessary for positive results. As well, a Black Box provides a reliable scientific control, with a high probability of success, from which to begin training in mental visualization. Whether the machine works on its own, or if it works because one believes it works, is not known.

One engineer reported that a physics instructor from a local university bought in a Black Box and demonstrated how it worked. After a successful demonstration the instructor removed the back of the machine and showed that the circuitry had been removed and in its place was a circuit diagram drawn on a piece of white card. The wires from the input coil were attached to the edge of this card to coincide with the circuit diagram input and likewise with the output connection. The diagram included the standard symbol for a battery. Strangely, when the schematic battery symbol was erased, the machine would not work. When the symbol was put back in, it operated as before.

Black Boxes have been used by various people to detect the type and quantity of unknown materials. It has been used for detecting and diagnosing energy flaws in animals and plants, measuring vital signs of remote individuals, perform dowsing, chakra location and healing.

Who knows what new purposes may be discovered by individuals with open minds. Communication with other states of reality, finding lost objects or even people, communication or travel through time?

The future prospects for radionics, psionics and Black Boxes are hindered only by a lack of imagination from individuals who fail to look beyond the current "comfort zone" of scientific understanding. Only by daring to dream can we hope to find a new and better understanding of our world, our universe and the amazing scientific principles that are yet to be discovered.

Para-View Into Other Worlds

NOTE: The following chapter is from the book *Para-X Powers: Unleashing The PSI Within You!*

THERE is a fantastic ability with Para-X Powers that allows you to easily see into the past, present and even the future. This ability is as easy to accomplish as sitting down and turning on your High Definition television set. But your HDTV won't allow you to see hidden secrets from the past, nor will it allow you to see what others are thinking about right at this very moment. Plus, I doubt that your TV has the ability to catch glimpses of the many probabilities of the future.

This valuable technique derived from Para-X Powers is called The Para-Viewer and it uses the reflective and refractive properties of a sphere made of crystal or glass in order to receive transmissions from the astral worlds. Of course this device is better known as a crystal ball, but a Para-Viewer can also be any object that is shiny and reflective, a mirror, or a clear glass of water for example.

For centuries people have been using crystal balls in an attempt to get a look into the future. This is a form of fortune telling called Scrying. The stereotype of an old Gypsy woman using a crystal ball to cheat a customer out of his hard-earned money has become so ingrained upon society that most people automatically reject the idea that a crystal ball has any valid psychic uses at all.

But don't let the bad publicity turn you away from learning how to use this amazing and useful device. The Para-Viewer can become an important tool for your success in business, love and all sorts of other major decisions in your life.

Man has made a considerable advance on the road to Attainment. Self-development and self-initiation are beginning to play a much more prominent part than before. Man is no longer content to believe what he is told; he at last desires to know from his own experience. The Para-Viewer is a vital stepping-stone towards self-knowledge.

Crystal gazing, as a method for inducing visions, has been quite common among all peoples, in all times. Not only the crystal but many other objects are similarly used; in Australia the native priests use water and shining objects, or in some cases, flame. In New Zealand some of the natives use a drop of blood. The Fijians fill a hole with water, and gaze into it. Some South American tribes use the polished surface of a black stone. The Native Americans used water and shining bits of flint or quartz.

Your Para-Viewer

The first thing you need to do is to find a Para-Viewer that you like and are comfortable using. Some esoteric scholars insist that only pure quartz crystal can be used for psychic viewing. This is only true if you believe it to be true. Nowadays there are many different types of materials that are used to make "crystal" balls...each and every one of them will work for you if you believe it will. That is why it is important to find one that appeals to you. In fact, look for a Para-Viewer that draws you to it like a piece of metal to a magnet. Then you will know for certain that you have found the right one.

The Occult Teachings inform us that in addition to the Five Physical Senses possessed by man: Seeing; Feeling; Hearing; Tasting; and Smelling; each of which has its appropriate sense organ, every individual is also possessed of Five Astral Senses, which form a part of what is known to Occultists as the Astral Body. These Astral Senses, which are the astral counterparts of the five physical senses, operate upon what

Occultists call the Astral Plane, which is next above the Physical Plane, in the Sevenfold Scale of Planes. Just as do the Physical Senses operate upon the Physical Plane, so do the Astral Senses operate upon the Astral Plane. By means of these Astral Senses, one may sense outside objects without the use of the physical senses usually employed. And it is through this sensing by these Astral Senses, that the phenomenon of Para-Viewing becomes possible.

By the employment of the Astral Sense of Seeing, the Para-Viewer is able to perceive occurrences, scenes, etc., at a distance sometimes almost incredibly far; to see through solid objects; to see records of past occurrences in the Astral Ether; and to see Future Scenes thrown ahead in Time, like the shadows cast by material objects — "coming events cast their shadows before," you have heard. By the use of the Astral Sense of Hearing, he is able to sense sounds over immense distances and often after the passage of great periods of time, for the Astral vibrations continue for many years.

The Astral senses of Taste and Smell are seldom used, although there are abundant proofs of their existence. The Astral Sense of Feeling enables the Para-Viewer to become aware of certain occurrences on the Astral Plane, and to perceive impressions, mental and otherwise, that are being manifested at a distance.

The Astral Sense of Feeling may be explained as being rather a sense of "Awareness," than a mere "Feeling," inasmuch as the viewer, through its channel, becomes "aware" of certain occurrences, other than by Astral Sight or Hearing, and yet which is not "Feeling" as the word is used on the Physical Plane. It may be well called "Sensing" for want of a better name, and manifests in a vague consciousness or "awareness."

Still, we must not overlook the fact that there are many instances of true "feeling" on the Astral Plane, for instances, cases where the viewer actually "feels" the pain of another, which phenomena is commonly known as "sympathetic pains," "taking on the condition," etc., etc., and which are well known to all investigators as belonging to the phenomena of the Astral Senses.

How To Develop Yourself

The ability to Para-View lies dormant in every person. This means that the Astral Senses are present in everyone, and the possibility of their being awakened into activity is always present. The different degrees of power observable in different persons depend chiefly upon the degree of development rather than upon the comparative strength of the faculties. In some persons, of certain temperaments, the Astral Senses are very near the manifesting point at all times.

Flashes of what are considered to be "intuition," premonitions, etc., are really manifestations of Para-X Powers in some phase. In the case of other persons, on the other hand, the Astral Senses are almost atrophied, so merged in materialistic thought and life are these people. The element of Faith also plays an important point in this phenomenon, as it does in all occult phenomena, for that matter. That is to say, that one's belief tends to open up the latent powers and faculty in man, while a corresponding disbelief tends to prevent the manifestation.

A Para-Viewer can be any object that is shiny and reflective, a crystal sphere, a mirror, or a clear glass of water.

There is a very good psychological reason for this as all students of the subject well know. Belief and Disbelief are two potent psychological factors on all planes of action. Occultists know, and teach, that the Astral Senses and faculties of the human race will unfold as the race progresses, at which time that which we now call Para-X Power will be a common possession of all persons, just as the use of the physical senses are to the race at the present time. In the meantime, there are persons who, not waiting for the evolution of the race, are beginning to manifest this power in a greater or lesser degree, depending much upon favorable circumstances, etc.

There are many more persons in this stage of development than is generally realized. In fact many persons manifesting Para-X Power, occasionally, are apt to pass by the phenomena as "imagination," and "foolishness," refusing to recognize its reality.

Then, again, many persons manifest the power during sleeping hours, and dismiss the matter as "merely a dream," etc.

You may ask "how will I know when my psychic abilities with the Para-Viewer begin to work?"

Some people begin by a plunge, as it were, and under some unusual stimulus become able just for once to see some striking vision; and very often in such a case, because the experience does not repeat itself, the seer comes in time to believe that on that occasion he must have been the victim of hallucination. Others begin by becoming intermittently conscious of the brilliant colors and vibrations of the human aura; others find themselves with increasing frequency seeing and hearing something to which those around them are blind and deaf; others again see faces, landscapes, or colored clouds floating before their eyes in the dark, before they sink to rest; while perhaps the commonest experience of all is that of those who begin to recollect with greater and greater clearness what they have seen and heard on other planes during sleep.

While it is very difficult to lay down a set method of instruction in the development of your ability to use your Para-Viewer, there are some things that are generally important for anyone seeking to develop their Para-X Powers.

The first is concentration. You should cultivate the faculty of concentration, which is the power to hold the attention upon an object for some time. Very few possess this power, although they may think they do. The best way to develop concentration is to practice on some familiar and common object, such as a pencil, book, ornament, etc. Take up the object and study it in detail, forcing the mind to examine and consider it in every part, until every detail of the object has been observed and noted. Then lay the object aside, and a few hours after pick it up again and repeat the process, and you will be surprised to see how many points you have missed on the first trial, Repeat this until you feel that you have exhausted your object. The next day take up another object, and repeat the process.

Practicing this way will not only greatly develop the powers of Perception, but will also strengthen your powers of concentration in a manner which will be of great value to you in Para-X development.

The second point of development is visualizing. In order to visualize you must cultivate the faculty of forming mental pictures of distant scenes, places, people, etc., until you can summon them before you at will, when you place yourself in the proper mental condition.

Another plan is to place yourself in a comfortable position, and then make a mental journey to some place that you have previously visited. Prepare for the journey, and then mentally see yourself starting on your trip; then seeing all the intermediate places and points; then arriving at your destination and visiting the points of interest, etc.; and then returning home. Then, later try to visit places that you have never seen, in the same way. This is not clairvoyance, but is a training of the mental faculties for the exercise of the real power.

After you have developed yourself along the lines of concentration, and visualization as above stated, you may begin to practice Psychometry, as follows: Take a lock of hair; or handkerchief; or ribbon; or ring; belonging to some other person, and then press it against your forehead, lightly, closing your eyes, and assuming a receptive and passive mental state. Then desire calmly that you Psychometrize the past history of the object. Do not be in too much of a hurry, but await calmly the impressions.

After a while you will begin to receive impressions concerning the person owning the object pressed against your forehead. You will form a mental picture of the person, and will soon begin to receive impressions about his characteristics, etc.

You may practice with a number of objects, at different times, and will gradually develop the Psychometric power by such practice and experiments. Remember that you are developing what is practically a new sense, and must have perseverance and patience in educating and unfolding it.

Another form of Para-X development is that of tracing the past history, surroundings, etc., of metals, minerals, etc. The process is identical to that just described. The mineral is pressed against the forehead, and with closed eyes the person awaits the Psychometric impression.

Some who have highly developed the faculty have been able to describe the veins of mineral, metal, etc., and to give much valuable information regarding same, all arising from the psychic clue afforded by a sample of the rock, mineral, metal, etc. There are other cases of record, in which underground streams of water have been discovered by Psychometrists, by means of the clue given by a bit of earth, stone, etc., from the surface. In this, as in the other phase mentioned, practice, practice, practice, is the summing up of the instruction regarding development.

Look Into Your Para-Viewer

Now that you are ready to gaze for the first time into your Para-Viewer, you should select a quiet room where you will be entirely undisturbed, taking care that it is as far as possible free from mirrors, ornaments, pictures, glaring colors and the like, which may otherwise distract the attention.

This room should be of a comfortable temperature in accordance with the time of year, neither too hot nor too cold. Make sure to prevent any artificial light rays from being reflected in, or in any manner directly reaching your Para-Viewer. Keep any light source to your back. The room should not be dark, but rather shadowed, or charged with dull light, somewhat such as prevails on a cloudy or wet day.

The Para-Viewer should be placed on a table, or it may rest on a dark colored cloth. Just make sure that there are no undesirable reflections to disturb your viewing. Before beginning to experiment, remember that most frequently nothing will be seen on the first occasion, and possibly not for several sittings, though some sitters, if strongly gifted with psychic powers may be fortunate enough to obtain good results the very first time.

For your first few times, have no goals set, simply gaze calmly at the Para-Viewer. Do not be afraid of blinking your eyes, and do not stare, strain or tire the eyes. Some prefer making funnels of their hands, and gazing through them as this serves to shut out distracting light, and sights. (You can use your Para-Transmitter for this purpose).

If nothing is perceived during the first few attempts, do not despair or become impatient or imagine that you will never see anything. Using your Para-Viewer is like learning to ride a bike, you may fall off the first few times, but eventually you will succeed.

It has been recommended that beginners failing to get direct results then try to "visualize" something that they have already seen something familiar, such as a chair, a ring, a face, etc., and then turning to the Para-Viewer and try to reproduce it there. It is claimed that this practice will often gradually lead to actual "seeing" in the Para-Viewer.

The first signs of the actual "seeing" in the Para-Viewer comes in the form of a "cloudiness," or "milky-mist," which slowly resolves itself into a form, or scene, which slowly appears within your Para-Viewer. In some cases, the "misty" cloud deepens into a black one, from which the pictures appear.

The Para-Viewer shouldn't be used right after eating, and avoid alcoholic drinks before a session. Avoid any illicit drugs as well, as they darken the mind and allow for negative thoughts to breed uncontrollably. The proper state of mind when using the Para-Viewer is extremely important. Mental anxiety, or ill health will play havoc with your sessions, so if you do not feel good, postpone your Para-Viewer session until later.

Some experts say that when you do start to see images within your Para-Viewer as a general rule, visions appearing in the extreme background indicate the far past or far future. While those images seen neared to the front denote the present or immediate future.

This question of "time" is an important one, and it is unfortunate that it should largely depend on your hunch. Time on other planes of reality is different from our own time. Since time is a mode of the human mind, and our mind is at a different state of vibration when examining a vision, the question is can you discern what "time" you are actually looking at? I think the best rule with this is to depend on your first impressions as these usually are correct. As you become more proficient at reading your Para-Viewer you will just "know" what you are looking at and at what "time" it is taking place.

Understanding Symbols

You will see two principal types of visions with your Para-Viewer: (1) The Symbolic, indicated by the appearance of symbols such as a flag, boat, knife, gold, etc.: and (2) Actual scenes and people, in action or otherwise.

Symbols are thought-forms which convey, by the association of ideas, a definite meaning in regard to the mind that generates them. They depend upon the laws of thought, and the correspondence that exists between the spiritual and material worlds, between the subject and the object of our consciousness.

All symbols, therefore, may be translated by reference to the known nature, quality, and uses of the objects they represent. Thus an arm will signify defense, power, protection; a mouth speech, revelation; an ear news, information; if distorted, scandal, abuse. The sun, shining brightly, denotes prosperity, honors. The moon, when crescent denotes success, increase, and improvement. When gibbous, it denotes sickness, losses, and trouble. The sun eclipsed shows death or ruin of a man; the moon, similarly afflicted, denotes equal danger to a woman. These are natural interpretations.

Symbols are almost infinite in number, and the interpretation of them requires unprejudiced skill, but they are nevertheless an important subject for study, and the use of the Crystal or Mirror by a positive seer can hardly be beneficial without a profound understanding of this subject. Although every symbol has some general signification in agreement with its natural qualities and uses, yet it obtains a particular meaning in relation to the individual. This is also the case in dreams, where every person is a natural seer. Few, however, pay that attention to dreams which their source and nature warrant. The Para-Viewer is but a means of bringing the normal dreaming faculty into conscious activity.

No definite rule can be laid down as to the interpretation of visions. The answers are actually within you. Your own personal symbols, as interpreted by your subconscious mind, are what you will end up viewing. If you associate airplanes with having to travel a great distance because of a death in the family, then when you see the image of an airplane in your Para-Viewer you are going to think of death and sorrow.

How To Travel To Other Dimensions

If you associate roller skating with meeting your first girl or boy friend, then if you experience a vision of people roller skating in your Para-Viewer, you are going to think of love and romance. So pay attention to how these images make you feel deep inside when you see them. Chances are the feelings; the very emotions that these symbols evoke within you are going to be the correct interpretations.

Woman Finds Lost Pet With Para-Viewer

One person who became convinced that her Para-Viewer did actually work was Annie G. of Nashville, Tennessee. Annie had been drawn to a small, glass ball that she found at an antique store. Right away she bought it, even though she really didn't need it. Later that week, Annie's beloved pet cat was accidentally let out of her apartment.

Annie was heartbroken and several days went by with no sign of her cat. Following the instructions on how to use a Para-Viewer, Annie sat down in a shaded room and concentrated on seeing her cat within her small, glass sphere.

Annie soon entered into a light trance state and her entire focus was on her little Para-Viewer. From within the clear, shiny ball, Annie could see an image slowly forming, it was the front entrance of a nearby convenience store.

She rushed to the store, and there was her cat. The owners had found her cat and were trying to find its owner. Somehow her Para-Viewer showed her a literal image on where Annie could find her cat. Annie's Para-Viewer was no fancy expensive crystal ball, but it worked just as well.

Para-Viewer Finds Money

Jake S. was a construction worker until the recent economic hardships, especially in the housing market, forced Jake's company to lay him off. With a family to take care of, Jake was uncertain what to do next.

Jake decided to put together his own Para-Viewer using a clear drinking glass filled with fresh water. He sat in a dark room with the glass in front of him and a small candle placed several feet away and to the right of the glass.

The first time Jake sat and looked into the glass for ten minutes. He grew tired and bored and gave up for the rest of the day. Late that night, Jake woke up and could not go back to sleep. He decided that since he was already awake and didn't have anything else to do, he would give his Para-Viewer another try. This time, however, almost as soon as he sat down in front of the glass, unusual images seem to float before his eyes from deep within the water.

As the images took shape, Jake recognized an old car, a Chevy, that his parents had owned when he was a child. He always associated his late father with that car as it had been his father's favorite and the two of them would spend the weekend's together working on it in their old garage.

Jake could not understand what his father's old car had to do with his need for money. His father had passed away years before and the car was long gone. He decided to visit his old childhood home, now abandoned and marked to be torn down, and see if he could find anything that could help him out.

Jake wandered through his old home, but nothing of any significance stood out to him. He then went out to the old garage to look around. The garage was completely empty and Jake was about to leave when he noticed something written on the wall. It was both his and his father's signatures along with a date from years ago. Jake remembered that they had signed the wall in celebration after successfully rebuilding the carburetor of the old Chevy.

Jake fondly brushed his hand across the old writing, and when he did the board shifted and came away from the wall. Inside the space was a yellowed envelope with Jake's name written on it in his father's handwriting. Opening the envelope, Jake found a large amount of cash, enough to keep his family going until he could find a new job. Jake has no idea when or why his father had hidden the money, but, if it hadn't been for the image seen in his Para-Viewer, he never would have found the money that his father had tucked away for him years ago.

A Few Helpful Hints

This section, while giving as much information as possible in the space allowed, aims to be intensely practical and helpful to all who may read it. Some will be at one stage of development, others will have reached a different level, but the author trusts that all will obtain some hints that may actually be put into practice, and thus lead the seeker to a clearer and better understanding of himself and others.

Here are a few practical hints:

A diet of fruit and vegetables may have its advantages by making the student more susceptible to visions of a clairvoyant type. On the other hand a mixed diet suits some people far better, and may give more real staying power. Don't become a "diet crank" you will have no time for anything else more important. Use your common sense – experiment if you like – but don't form habits. The best type of man or woman is the one who can eat anything, and does eat anything according to the natural promptings of his or her being, and that without causing digestive troubles.

Don't do any practice after a full meal, or when very tired; this would not be giving Nature a proper chance, and your practice must suffer accordingly.

Rather be the tortoise than the hare. Real progress is made despite obstacles, and the more obstacles we meet, and overcome, the stronger our will becomes.

You are practically bound to obtain what you truly ask for. Be sure of what you really want before you ask for it.

Take plenty of fresh air and exercise, and don't become so obsessed with dark séances that you overlook the value of Sunlight.

Your first duty to Humanity is self-improvement. Man is ignorant of the nature and powers of his own being. Until he has obtained a scientific knowledge of himself, he cannot really expect to aid others.

It requires much more study and effort to Know Yourself, than it does to give others advice they do not need.

Learn to mind your own business, and in time others will follow your example.

Learn to speak the truth, and you will begin to notice when you are telling lies. Remember that even truth is relative. There is but one Truth and that lies at the End of the Path. Yet seek Truth, and be content with nothing less.

We live in a world of appearances. There seem to be innumerable, "Pairs of Opposites" till the final Pair has been realized and mated. Then we shall "See things as they are."

How To Travel To Other Dimensions

Other Worlds Await

Many people on the metaphysical path are stretching themselves to encompass a broader vision that embraces the realities of Earth with the knowledge of the universe. Within this is the desire to reestablish contact with our cosmic brothers and sisters in other dimensions and realities.

The ancient Atlantian's had developed methods to leave the planet through the use of dimensional and time portals. By knowledge and use of the cycles of time, Atlantian's could connect with and even travel to other dimensions with ease on a single and properly applied breath.

Unfortunately, this ancient method has been lost to us through the passage of time. We are now just starting to relearn the incredible powers and energies that are available to us when we learn to control our minds and channel the universal energies properly.

One exciting way to reconnect ourselves to the cosmos is called the universal mer-ka-ba meditation, and comes to us from Aluna Joy Yaxk'in – It is preferable to do this outside standing on the earth and barefoot, under the stars. Stand with back straight. Become aware of yourself. Become aware of the universe. Now envision yourself inside a brilliant tetrahedral pyramid of transparent light. All you can see are the straight edges of the triangle form.

Envision your head is the capstone of the pyramid. Make the boundaries of the pyramid grow and grow until you are as tall as the tallest tree, then the tallest mountain . . . and now your head is reaching the boundaries of Earth's atmosphere. You are inside the Earth-based tetrahedral pyramid.

This pyramid contains the frequencies of life on earth, its history and influences of its inhabitants. Now look up and see an upside down, brilliantly transparent, cosmic tetrahedral pyramid descending to you. This tetrahedral pyramid contains wisdom, truth and pure radiant light of the universe. Stretch your arms up to the stars making an upside down triangle above you. This makes a place for this cosmic pyramid to merge with the Earth based tetrahedral pyramid.

Consciously pull this tetrahedral pyramid to you. Pull it to you until the apex of the cosmic pyramid is touching the top of the Earth's tetrahedral pyramid (your crown chakra). Slowly pull the cosmic tetrahedron into your being until the top point of the Universal pyramid descends past your feet, into the earth, and down to the Earth's core.

You have now anchored the universal frequencies with Earth's frequencies within your human body. In this space, realize you are a cosmic being. You always have been. You are a child of the universe . . . but somewhere you just forgot. Affirm you remember the wisdom of the universe and that all natural states of being human are fully restored.

In this cosmic state of awareness take some time to listen with your cosmic ears. Listen to the song of the stars and Moon. Be aware that you are not alone on Earth or in this universe. Be open to the presence of your cosmic brothers and sisters. These are the ones who star seeded you. They are your family and they miss you as much as you miss them. Listen to their message.

Now go beyond all personality, and listen to the song of the universe. This song cannot be sung by one being. It can only be sung by the collective whole. It is indescribable, nearly audible and when you experience it you will hear and feel the frequency of the universal whole.

Remember that you are a part of this song. Your cosmic brothers and sisters are here to guide you and it is your responsibility to once again re-anchor the universal light of truth and wisdom to the Earth plane. This is why we are here. Now radiate the light and knowledge that is within you, and encourage others to follow.

How To Travel To Other Dimensions

This simple exercise can be done at sunrise or sunset, under the moon in its different phases, or under the stars, or even looking out a window. When you have practiced this enough, it only needs to take a few seconds to stay in sync with the universe. It is as simple as looking up and realizing we are children of the universe.

We have found a way of separating the spirit and the subconscious from the human body and the conscious. Our spirit is as free as the wind and can travel to many places.

Cruise The Universe With Your Astral Body

The sensation of having an existence separate from one's physical body, and even being able to stand outside of oneself is a strange but common paranormal experience. Out of body experiences (OOBEs) cannot be dismissed as mere hallucination or fantasy, because often a person has been seen by others while traveling in his or her astral body. Sometimes the cosmic traveler has acquired information from a physically remote location thereby proving that the experience was real.

The astral plane is another dimension, or a parallel universe, as a scientist would say. The astral plane is the dimension where each one of us goes every time we sleep, with our astral body. It is the land of dreams. Every night in our dreams we repeat to a greater or lesser degree our daily events, thoughts and feelings. These are often transformed by our psyche into the most ludicrous or fantastic scenarios. Our subconscious projects them into the astral environment, and this is generally how our dreams are created.

This process is what clouds our perception of the real astral environment, in much the same way as a daydream stops us from perceiving our physical environment. Nonetheless, we may sometimes wake in the morning, recalling dreams of places we've never been before. It is very likely that we visited the astral counterpart of that physical place, even if it was in a hazy, dreamlike state.

Within the astral plane there exists all that exists in the physical plane. However, there is much in the astral plane that we could never find in the physical: incredible worlds, divine beings, amazing phenomenon.

But sadly, those unconscious thoughts and feelings, many of which we are unaware during the day, are recollected by the subconscious and projected into the astral realm at night, making either our dream experiences too vague or blocking out the reality of where we are all together. Astral travel is very different to normal dreaming. It is an extraordinary experience. All who have experienced it can testify to its lucidity and magical quality.

It is interesting that conscious astral travel is experienced as clearly as we experience our daily life. In fact, it is even experienced more clearly at times: our senses seem sharper and the environment somehow more real.

It is often considered that astral travel (out-of-body experiences) is only encountered by people that have had a near death experience after an accident or on the operating table. But astral travel is a natural possibility that anyone can develop through practice.

In the astral the sky is not the limit. One can fly way beyond the blue sky, into deep space exploring the planets. One can consciously project to any part of the world through concentration.

We can fly through the air, having a birds eye view of what is below, traveling across the surface of our huge planet. Imagine being able to glide over the ocean like a seagull, or being able to penetrate into it and breath beneath it like a fish. We can meet enlightened beings, even of distant ancient traditions, who can help guide us along the spiritual path. Or we can even attend true esoteric schools and temples to learn much about the mysteries of life and death.

There is all sorts of hidden knowledge one can acquire through astral projection, knowledge that cannot be acquired in everyday life, from other people or books. This is the reason why many want to astral travel – to acquire knowledge through experience about ourselves, about the Earth, the universe, etc.

All of this is available to us through astral travel. It is something worth experiencing and verifying.

It's Not As Difficult As You May Think

It is easy to learn how to travel the astral planes of existence. There are a number of methods available for your experimentation. However, you will find that only one or two methods work best for you. It is advisable for you to try several methods to find which works for you. Here are a couple of methods that most people find easy to work.

Step 1. - Before dropping off to sleep, put your body into a deep state of relaxation. Do this by systematically tensing and relaxing each muscle one at a time. Start with the toes and work up the body to the face. This will put your body into such an unfamiliar deep state of relaxation that in the early days you may feel a little discomfort. Your body may feel unbearably heavy but there's nothing to worry about.

Step 2. - Now let your breathing become slow and deep. Slow, deep breathing will relax you further and keep you alert. Focus your attention on the center of your forehead but don't fall asleep.

Step 3. - Become aware of just how heavy your body feels. Think of it as cumbersome and made of clay. Now set your attention on your astral duplicate body. See it as made of light. It is weightless and free. Picture in your mind's eye images of bubbles, sunlight, feathers floating on the breeze, smoke rising upwards. Your body is heavy but your soul is weightless.

Step 4. - At this point many people report of being able to 'see' the darkened room even though their eyes are closed. It appears to be bathed in a purple light. If you get this far, try to focus your attention on the ceiling light fitting.

Step 5. - Imagine drawing the light bulb toward you. As you do this, you may feel yourself floating toward the ceiling. Try to remain conscious. You will become aware of floating in your astral self and may even see your sleeping body laid below you on the bed.

Another good method is called **The Moving Anchor**. After meditating into a state of total deep relaxation, imagine an object about six feet in front of your eyes. Now feel this object pulling at you like a magnet. Once you can see the object clearly in your minds eye and feel the pull of the object on you, begin to move the object slowly toward you. Just a small amount at first. As the object moves toward you feel the pull getting stronger. Now move it back again (the pull gets weaker as you do). Now repeat the process moving the object closer each time and feeling the pull becoming stronger and stronger as the object comes closer.

Once you are comfortable with the movement of the object begin the process again, only this time the movement of the object should be a fluid motion, and as the object moves to and fro it should be like a wave. You should also feel this wave on yourself as the pull gets stronger and weaker and stronger again.

Finally as the object virtually reaches you the strength of the pulling force combined with the wave like motion will simply pull you right out of your physical body.

One more excellent and easy method is to simply lay down

with the lights off. Make sure you are completely relaxed. Lie there and be quite and still, calm and clear your mind. Imagine your astral body which may look like grey matter shaped in the form of your body. Imagine it lifting and floating out of your body, floating up to the ceiling in your room. Turn and look down and try to see you body lying there.

If you are successful, you may want to stay in the room and float around a bit, staying close to the body. Or you can choose to walk through walls and travel to wherever you wish to go. You can fly there or you can will yourself there instantly.

Just remember when trying to astral project: You need to be calm and very relaxed. You should not be over full in the stomach or feeling hungry. Practice only when your mind can be focused. Make sure the room temperature is comfortable. Do not get too excited or fired up. Stay balanced. People who are having relationship problems usually have difficulty in projecting.

One Dragonstar student by the name of Susan relates her personal experience with astral travel.

The concept of astral travel seemed to me to be a waste of time. I was set in my beliefs that such practices were difficult to prove and had no true purpose except to disorientate people. It wasn't until I began to have unusually clear dreams that my interest in astral travel developed. At one point my dreams became so vivid that they seemed real. I thought I was in the physical world, until I woke up to find myself in my bedroom. On other occasions I knew I was not in the physical but in the astral plane, without having prior knowledge of this dimension.

Suddenly all my beliefs were turned on their head. Something had now changed within me. I gradually started to accept the possibilities that there were unknown realities and times that existed beyond what my physical eyes could see, and what my physical body could sense. I went along to many spiritual fairs, and I read and heard other people's teachings on the correct method to successfully astral project. All the theories were filled with complicated techniques and occult jargon. I had no hope of understanding the theory, let alone the practices. I felt intimidated, and I started to believe that astral travel was only possible for adepts and spiritual masters.

It wasn't until I came across the teachings of Dragonstar, which eventually led me to a genuine astral experience. I remember being stunned at the simplicity of the astral technique. Any questions I had were answered clearly and from personal experience. This was the impetus for me to start practicing regularly.

When one thing didn't work for me, I would try something else. For instance I found that doing the practice at night was unsuccessful. I was usually tired after work, and I would fall asleep and miss the all-important astral split. This is the moment during the practice where you need to be aware of your astral body splitting from your physical body. I decided to try the practice when I was well rested, and on a sunny weekend, in the comfort of my living room. It was an idea I had which I felt would help, and it did. Eventually I had a genuine astral experience. It took me a good twelve months of continual effort to get it right. Fear and ignorance was a major obstacle that I had to overcome.

The theory I heard and read, about experiencing a buzzing sound in the head as you astral project, became a reality for me. I also realized how far this theory, although correct, was from direct experience. It's like trying to explain to somebody, the feeling you get when you sky dive from an airplane. People can only imagine what it's like, until they have enough courage to try it for themselves. I can speak about the astral plane from personal experience now, and I don't have to cling with my imagination to unfounded theory, which although helps to get you started, is only a means to an end.

You can discover a magical world, much lighter and freer than the physical plane. You can see aspects of yourself that are impossible to see in the physical world. You can have insights into your own psyche and personality, and you can discover more about yourself, and how you exist in the world. If you learn to stay awake in the astral plane long enough, you can call real spiritual masters, who can give you intimate spiritual teachings, that relate to your own secret spiritual path.

It may all sound very far away and weird, but I was a hard skeptic once, and now I have seen the results for my self. The metaphysical world can be intimidating at first, because it's not a place people are used to going to consciously. I encourage anybody who has an interest in this area to give it a go, and to keep trying the practices, until you get even the smallest result. The experience will open your eyes to the bigger picture of life. It can really be life changing. You will be amazed at what you can discover.

The Wonders Of Time Travel

Time, with its relentless passageway through our lives, appears impossible to conquer or even tame. Yet, despite the overwhelming odds against it, we all have the innate desire to change our past and know our future. It is as if we know, deep-down within the core of our souls, that time is not so insurmountable after all. That time as we know it, does not really exist.

For your astral self, time travel is real and possible. When you project your astral body, you can journey into the past, present or future, and come back whenever you are ready. This easy method will take you through time by means of the astral planes and visualization. Your physical body will remain safe at home – it is your astral self that will travel and interact with time.

Some people, after mastering astral time travel, have reported that they have learned to send their physical body across time and space. However, this is a feat that should not be attempted by the novice. Reports of people mysteriously disappearing forever could be the result of accidental activation of this time-bending ability.

Before you start, practice your favorite meditation technique. If you cannot meditate then you will have no success with this type of time travel. You must be able to go into your meditative state and clear your mind of all outside thoughts and distractions. This is an exercise that is best done in private. Please make sure that you can practice in a quiet room absent of any bother.

As you meditate, imagine a building in the middle of a field or in the middle of nowhere surrounded by nothing. You will use this same building every time you practice. The building can be any shape or size. Many imagine their very own pyramid. Your building should have no windows, this way you will not be disturbed by anything on the "outside."

The inside of this building can be as simple or as plush as you wish it to be. The simpler it is, however, the fewer distractions you will have. Just make sure it is the same every time you practice.

Imagine that inside this building will be a room where you have a chair. This chair, a big black recliner with controls built into the arm, is a special chair. These controls are buttons that will take you where you want to go. You may set up these buttons in any configuration. For instance – a past button – a present button – and a future button. For even more control, try a LED display with a number key pad for punching in the exact year in time you wish to travel. If you do not want to use a chair, you may imagine some big elaborate machine with all the same controls.

In this room will also be a giant movie screen. This screen is where you will be watching the time frame you have chosen. Try to think of how you want all these items – the building – the time machine – the screen – before you actually go into meditation. Predetermine how you want them all to look beforehand.

Go into your meditative state. When you are totally relaxed take a mental walk to your special building and close the door. Sit in your special chair or machine and relax for a few more minutes. When you are ready, push the button that makes your screen come down from the ceiling and just sit there and stare at it for a minute. Now, dial in what time period and where you travel. Do not try to force this to happen, you must remain patient for the screen to come on. If you are impatient, it will not happen. Your mind must be receptive to what is being shown. It may take several days of trying before you actually see anything but, it will happen.

When you want to come back . . . just push the buttons for the present on your chair and take a few minutes to evaluate everything you saw. Then when you are ready get up out of your chair and walk out of the building and back to your physical body.

As you practice this method, you will soon find that you no longer need the building, the time machine or the screen. These are mental constructions to help you learn how it "feels" to travel through time. Once you have learned how to do this, you can travel back and forth through time as effortlessly as going to sleep at night.

As you travel through time, you can actually take part again in your past triumphs and attempt to fix your mistakes and failures. You can even see the possible realities that are created by your efforts. You can even travel to and occupy one of these other realities for as short or as long as you want. It makes no difference because you can return to your body seconds after you left. Time has no meaning to the astral plane.

This method can also be used to have the Ascended Masters show you things you need to learn. Just go through the same process and ask the Masters to show you on the screen what you want to know.

Another method that is very popular with students of the paranormal is to lie back on your bed in a comfortable position, gently close your eyes and relax. Letting go of any pain take slow, deep comfortable breaths through the nose.

Without worry or fear, clear your mind of distracting thoughts. You can focus on your breath or chant a favorite mantra. Imagine you're in an elevator moving upwards. Vividly feel the upwards motion.

Now relax completely to that point between sleep and consciousness, keep focused on the image and feeling of moving up. Tell yourself you will wake up fully out of the body. Imagine you are rising up from your body and drift off to sleep.

To move in time: Focus very vividly on the time you want to journey. Feel what is happening at that very moment. You will experience the feeling of moving very rapidly through the air.

How To Travel To Other Dimensions

Some report the feelings of moving through water or very dense gas. You may catch glimpses of your past and future as you travel. Stay focused on where you want to go. The slightest distraction will send you off into a completely different direction.

When you arrive at your destination, you may have trouble focusing on what is going on around you. This is often reported by first-timers to the world of time travel. The sensations that you are now able to perceive can be overwhelming and even frightening. Not only will you be aware of your own feelings and thoughts, you will also be aware of what everyone else is thinking as well. When the sensations become too intense, it is time for you to return to try again some other time.

When you have learned that time is meaningless to you – you are free to travel when and wherever you want in this universe. However, with this ability comes great responsibility. If your purpose is to try and change the past, you should realize that changing the past could affect your present life for the worse.

Most often, on your return, nothing will seem to have happened. Other times you will find yourself in a present that is completely different from the world you left. This is because with every change of your past, new and different realities are created. You may find yourself occupying a new world with no desire to return to the world that you left behind.

The astral plane has numerous dimensions of existence, and contains life in abundance. However, we are free to travel not only in the astral worlds, but as we stated before, through time space and the infinite worlds of probability. So come along and allow my co-author, S. Panchadasi to guide you to the mysterious worlds of existence that await those brave enough to take the ultimate journey.

144

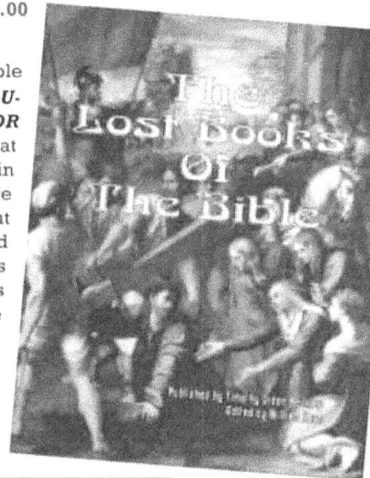

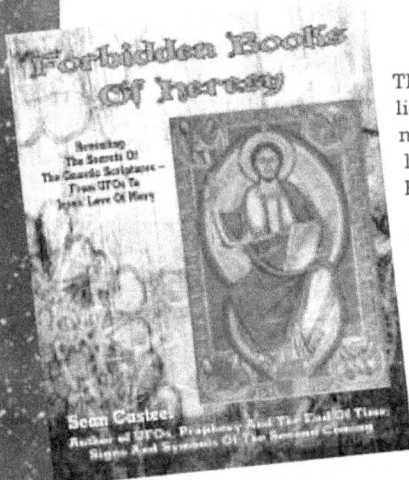

www.ingramcontent.com/pod-product-compliance
Lightning Source LLC
LaVergne TN
LVHW061224060426
835509LV00012B/1411